? 145

? 168

181 - "56"

# Life, Death,
## and
# Beyond Smiggle's Bottom

187 ?

199

201 !

208            Ō

230 SKA   ska

(dotage)? rigid in my ←

↳ "mental decline
of the aged"

# Life, Death,
## and
# Beyond Smiggle's Bottom

Gay Partington Terry

Cover & Design: Greg Salisbury
Editing: Deb Coman
Typesetting: Greg Salisbury

# Dedication

For the descendants: Travis and Zoe, Adriana, Evan, Landon, Nola, and Callum. For Becky and Mike who complete (and expand) the cast. And especially for Howie, my partner in this (and other) fantasies.

√

# Testimonials

*"Felicity is an unforgettable character whose blow-your-mind fantasy world is like nothing I have ever read. "LIFE, DEATH AND BEYOND SMIGGLE'S BOTTOM" is hilarious and also might make you shed a tear or two. I could not put the book down. There is a great movie or TV series herein".*

**—Lloyd Kaufman, President, Troma Entertainment and Creator of "THE TOXIC AVENGER"**

*"LIFE, DEATH AND BEYOND SMIGGLE'S BOTTOM" is a wonderful story... rich in interesting characters and thoughtful observations about life. Gay does a wonderful job of connecting where we come from to where we are and the different choices we make as we navigate through life. The contrast, as an example, between Felicity's early life in western Pennsylvania with her adult life in college and then again in Manhattan is so compelling that it can send the reader's thoughts into her or his own memories of leaving home and making a life.*

*The use of funeral experiences acts as a wonderful cultural translator that focuses on family and traditions. Seeing the experience through Felicity's eyes as a child explains much about her development as a person.*

*"LIFE, DEATH AND BEYOND SMIGGLE'S BOTTOM" is a heartfelt read, sparking reflections by reader's of the trials and wonderment of their journey through life."*

**—Dr. Michael H. Glantz, Director of Consortium for Capacity Building, University of Colorado, Boulder**

"Gay Terry has a unique, superb voice the likes of which you have not encountered before. *"LIFE, DEATH AND BEYOND SMIGGLE'S BOTTOM"* has a brilliant sense of prose, humor, and philosophy. It may or may not be fiction, and may or may not be speculation, but it all rings true. Terry dwells on death for the majority of the book, but never in a maudlin or creepy manner — in fact it, is often downright funny."

— Jim Freund, host of WBAI's "Hour of the Wolf"

"From the backwoods of Western Pennsylvania coal country to the spires of New York City sophistication, with stops along the way where fact and fantasy mingle (sometimes hard to tell apart), Gay Partington Terry's new book, *"LIFE, DEATH AND BEYOND SMIGGLE'S BOTTOM"*, is a pure delight! A wonderful story teller with a wonderful story to tell!"

— David "The Wizard" Bennett Cohen, original keyboardist for Country Joe and the Fish.

# Acknowledgements

I want to thank the Universe and its Creator for the incredible journey provided to me—the sharp turns and steep hills; the traffic, the views, bumpy rides, smooth sailing, moments of stillness and chaos. This book is about sunsets and sunrises (in that order). It took years to write it and a lifetime of experiences real and…well, real to me.

Many thanks to Greg Salisbury and Deb Colman. To the women in my writing group and to other friends who supported me: Bert, Patti, Linda. Thanks to my teachers (they know who they are), family (see above) and Howie again and again and again…

*? his degree in ?*

# Contents

"Some stories are true that never happened." Elie Wiesel

SOME STORIES AND CHARACTERS HAVE BEEN ADAPTED, EXPANDED, EXAGGERATED, AND COMBINED IN ORDER TO PROTECT THE INNOCENT, THE NOT-SO-INNOCENT, AND THE JUST PLAIN DAMNED. SOME HAPPENED PURELY IN MY HEAD ...

# Preface

The clicking you hear is the sound of wind slapping the rope against the flagpole. The caretaker's gone home; he leaves every day at four. Everyone else in this cemetery is dead. I come to watch the sunset. The people on this hill have the best view in town. Of course the price they pay for this view is unfortunate.

I sit near Mrs. Prospero, beneath the shade of her Aspen tree. Mrs. Prospero died in 1904 at the age of sixty-seven. She lies near her husband who died fifteen years before her. They do not share a stone. Aside from her name and dates, her stone tells us she is "at rest." I believe there's an intriguing story behind Mrs. Prospero. She must have toiled mercilessly during her sixty-seven years, for all that was left to say about her was "at rest." This tells me that there were way too many complications in her life to put on a stone. (Many people here have wonderfully succinct histories on theirs). Also, it's possible that she had a traumatic marriage as she lived fifteen years alone rather than take on another man. This was probably not out of love as she wasn't willing to share a stone with her husband like most others here—especially the older inhabitants (including my own parents).

My other concern regarding Mrs. Prospero is, who was responsible for the epitaph "at rest." There's no notation on her stone that she was "beloved mother," or "beloved grandmother." So, if there was a child or children, then it's possible she was not "beloved." Perhaps, she was so busy toiling that her children were neglected, or her husband was abusive and she was unable to protect the children. But if this was true, she would surely not have been buried near him. Some stones say "beloved sister," "beloved child." Mrs. Prospero's parents were likely deceased before her but I can find no evidence of her parents, siblings, or other family members in this cemetery, as her maiden name isn't given. Perhaps she moved away from them when she married or emigrated from another country. Perhaps her marriage was arranged at a distance.

It's probable that she commissioned the stone herself before death; the practice isn't uncommon here-about. If this is so, then she didn't feel "beloved." It's possible she was looking forward to some rest after a difficult life.

Mrs. Prospero and I have enjoyed many fine sunsets together and are thankful for the shade of the Aspen tree, which was certainly here when she purchased the plot as it's positively ancient. Mrs. Prospero's plot is not only a pleasant place to watch sunsets, but a convenient place to rest after visiting my own family members who are buried in this cemetery. I don't know any of Mrs. Prospero's family and I have no emotional attachment to Mrs. Prospero. Her tree offers shade and support, and her view toward the living is excellent. My mother, father, grandfather, and a dear friend of my grandmother (who I'll discuss later) are buried on the knoll above. They have no tree but are near the cottage where the caretaker lives. The caretaker, Mr. Beardsley, is the son of Old Mr. Beardsley who was caretaker before him and knew my father and grandmother. He's unmarried (as you might imagine an only child who grew up in such a "grave" environment might be) and disposed to conversation. I don't come here for graveyard chitchat or funereal gossip—not that it isn't interesting and often fascinating, albeit often disrespectful. It's my preference to avoid the imposition of such a person, though I do have sympathy for his circumstance.

If not for Beardsley's intrusions, I'm quite at home here. I'm not inordinately uncomfortable around death these days, though it's not a condition I care to stalk. I've become familiar with its disruptive impact and both its gentle and violent aspects.

I've felt the world recede and the particle that is me all but disappear a few times in this life, and resolved to take what evasive action I can. When you're young, it's difficult to recognize your own mortality and you worry more about losing others.

If you have a good mother, you aren't afraid for yourself.

# Chapter 1

## Riding off into the sunset

The first funeral I attended was for Uncle Walter, my mother's oldest brother. (There were three more uncles and four aunts on my mother's side—don't try to keep them straight.) It was in the early Fifties, so I was about seven or eight. My dad said Uncle Walter was a drunk, but he wasn't a philosophical Jackie Gleason drunk (the only kind I knew of at that time). He was just loudly happy and a little sloppy.

My mother's family didn't fly; nobody we knew had ever been in an airplane back then. We had to wait for people to drive up from Maryland and southern Virginia and find us in the wilds of southwest Pennsylvania. Aunt Kat and Uncle James and their kids never did make it from Kansas. Uncle Walter had to lie in a box for a week with family and friends hovering about in various stages of remorse/grief/hysteria—not that I knew anything about grief then or learned much about it from that experience. I was not very close to Uncle Walter; all I felt was confusion and curiosity.

The ladies fussed with their stockings and girdles, shared recipes, and gossiped. The women on both sides of my family were the kind of women who'd spend hours embroidering polyester pillowcases or tatting lace on baby clothes from Sears.

I do very little that's constructive.

The workingmen got there in the evenings and spent most of their time smoking cigarettes outside. They didn't talk nearly as much as the women. We kids could play on the big porch or the steps in the front of Mr. Wojtonowski's Funeral Home, or in the yard--as long as we were quiet. If we got out of hand we had to go inside and sit in the room with Uncle Walter, and be scared into silence by the presence of death.

Gram was a much bigger problem than us kids. She was angry. Angry at Aunt Anne, Walter's wife, for reasons I never understood. Angry at Mr. Wojtonowski for giving Uncle Walter a back room. (Mr. Friguglietti got the big room because he had more relatives than Gram and his son was Mr. Wojtonowski's garbage man.) Angry at my mother for using this time to try and make peace between various factions of the family. Angry at Uncle Walter for dying before she did. It was the only time I ever saw Gram that angry; she was usually a patient and resigned woman. But she even dressed down the Almighty a couple of times that week.

The room itself, though smaller than Mr. Friguglietti's, seemed cavernous. Uncle Walter lay at one end, surrounded by stands of flowers. Relatives congregated in the back. Occasionally one or two brave souls would venture up to "view" him, but kids never did this voluntarily. I'd never seen a dead body before and was curious but had to pretend to the other kids that I thought it was yucky. I could tell that there was nothing alive about the waxy thing in the box but didn't think it was yucky like roadkill, which the other kids found fascinating.

After I looked in the box, I could never remember Uncle Walter alive. I can't to this day.

Mr. Wojtonowski's funeral home was old, the sort of place you couldn't imagine as anything other than funereal even though it must have been some rich person's house at one time. It had high ceilings, rosewood moldings and sad wall paper with a raised texture you could barely make out because of wear; it's color was institutional green (as were all public spaces at the time). The spindly folding chairs looked incongruous in the room, and creaked ominously under the weight of lumpy mourners. Gram was the lumpiest of all, not fat, but shapeless. She never allowed anyone to see anything resembling a human form through her loose-fitting dresses. Her low-heeled old-lady shoes made just enough noise to let you know that she meant business. And she had the smell all old people had in those days, false teeth and mothballs, even though she was only in her sixties at that time.

AN EXAMPLE OF GRAM'S NO-NONSENSE ATTITUDE: SHE HAD A LOT OF PROBLEMS WITH HER TEETH SO WHEN SHE WAS A YOUNG MOTHER ON THE FARM, IN HER EARLY TWENTIES, SHE TOLD THE DENTIST, "JUST PULL ALL THESE TEETH OUT; I DON'T HAVE THE TIME OR MONEY FOR THEM." HE DID. AND BECAUSE OF RELIGIOUS BELIEFS, WHICH I'LL DISCUSS LATER, SHE REFUSED ANESTHESIA.

My cousins were all older, practically grown-ups, and didn't pay any attention to me, but I had invisible friends. "Only" children are resourceful. I kept to the corners, listening. The girl cousins were pretty boring; they talked about boys mostly, and school. The boys played ball in the yard till they got excited and noisy and someone yelled at them a couple of times, then they were stuck inside with the grown-ups, dead and alive. That shut them up.

JoeTom (or was his name Kenny?), who was someone's cousin and maybe eleven years old, took me aside and told me (with lurid details and demonstrations) about the blacksnake he killed with a hatchet. I learned later that blacksnakes were not harmful and even helpful, as they killed rats and mice. This was undoubtedly the first time a boy tried to impress me, a milestone. Though why anyone would try to impress a geeky eight year old at a funeral, is beyond me.

The grown-ups talked about Uncle Walter and how much he could drink and still seem normal. Like I said, once I saw him in the box, painted up and lifeless, I could never remember him alive so I don't remember what Uncle Walter's "normal" looked like. I know he fixed cars and that he must have been good at it because they had a nice house and his daughters, Ginger and Maybelle had uneven parallel bars in the yard. Uneven parallel bars were something people performed on in the Olympics, I was told by an older cousin. ("Don't you know anything, you dumb kid?") Ginger and Maybelle, and some of the other cousins could swing themselves around on them in a variety of Olympic-like configurations. I, on the other hand, got nauseous and dizzy skinning-the-cat on the shorter one and couldn't reach the higher one. Kids with asthma, like me, don't do gymnastics.

The grown-ups also said a lot of bad stuff about Aunt Anne,

that she might have been cheating on Uncle Walter, that she took money from people and didn't pay them back (which makes sense to me now in light of the fact that Uncle Walter was a raging alcoholic who spent his money buying drinks for himself and others). Aunt Anne was a small sad woman. She'd always been nervous so I couldn't imagine her fooling anyone about anything—that's what I knew about cheating. My dad told a story about how Aunt Anne sent him to get Uncle Walter late one afternoon when we were visiting. Uncle Walter had been drinking in a bar since morning. He told my dad to sit down and have a drink while he lined up five shots, drank them down and walked a straight line out of the bar. This story didn't impress me at the time, but I realize what a feat it is now. My mother's family was famous for its idiot savants—a few dim-witted hillbillies who had one quirky, but impressive, talent. Uncle Walter's was holding his liquor.

You can see where that gets you.

Gram stayed with us that week and my mom and I drove her to the funeral home every day. She didn't get up at five in the morning and make me apple dumplings like she usually did when she visited. She didn't bake bread or even crochet. I stayed pretty much away from her because of the anger thing. My invisible friends came in handy, as they did in a lot of situations. The relatives thought I was such a nice quiet child, but the invisibles and I were planning to take over the world, killing people off right and left, destroying stuff, blowing things up. Kerpow!

My mother didn't cook either that week. Neighbors brought us food. Most of it was in casseroles and had meat in it, so I wouldn't eat it. Nobody noticed, for a change, and I didn't have to sit at the table until I ate my one bite. They let me live on peanut butter and jelly for the whole week. We got some good cookies but Mrs. Whitney, next door, brought lemon meringue pie. Yuch! I hate meringue; it's just a mouth full of slime.

I don't remember the funeral. Did I even go? It's possible I stayed home with some of the cousins. It was the one thing I wanted to see most: the actual hole and how they lowered the box into it, what they said over it, who shoveled dirt into it after, what it would say on the stone and what all the other stones said. I had a great interest in funerals as I performed them quite often—for various pets belonging to friends, dead animals I found in the woods, even broken toys. I learned my rituals from TV and books, and embellished them with personal touches. Despite my lack of firsthand experience, all the neighborhood kids knew I was the one to call on for ceremonies.

Even though I was young, Uncle Walter's demise was not my first contact with death. Dead birds and pets are one thing, but I also had a clear memory of a violent death in another life. That is, I had the memory, but I didn't understand what it was for a long time.

~

My grandfathers were always dead. Well, I guess that's not entirely accurate, but from my point of view they were. Gram's husband, Asa Little, died of a stroke and left her with nine kids (three of them still at home) and a rented farm (the Poor Farm—as bad as that sounds, it's just that they leased the land from Mr. Poor—as opposed to the Teets Farm, the Gouker Farm, the Seese Farm, the Wilde Farm—you get the picture). The oldest of the three younger kids was my mother, Rose Grace; I called her M. She quit high school and went to "beauty school" when her father died. Gram picked herself up, moved to town (Harrow, Pennsylvania) and opened a beauty

?gave

parlor. She and M fixed hair and give manicures so that Uncle
Edward and Aunt Kat could finish school. M quit working
when I was born but practiced on my hair until I went away to
college. She was always giving me new "dos" which I mostly
hated; I'm not a "do" sort of person. The worst was when I was
little and she put my hair up in rags so I'd have sausage curls
like Shirley Temple. I kind of liked the look of the curls when
they were finished, and how you could make them bounce, but
sleeping with the tight rags hurt. It took hours to get them in
and they had to be real tight and painful to make the curls.
"Beauty must suffer," she'd say.

Fuck beauty, I say.

The truth about Gram and Asa Little's family is that they
were in this country a long time, hundreds of years—well,
at least one hundred. They came from places like Northern
Ireland and England as indentured servants and worked their
way up to become tenant farmers. They were poor, but mostly
upstanding folk. Farmers are middle-class where I come from.
In the years the Little's were here they married everybody--
everybody they could find
in Northern Appalachia:
Dutch, Welsh, Slavic, even
a Seneca Indian. They drew
the line at Italians which is
sad because it certainly could
have improved the bloodline
and Sunday dinners.

There was only one photo
(a tiny daguerreotype) of
Grandpa Asa and I got hold
of it once and took it to a
photographer friend who

blew it up for me. This was after I'd gone to college and taken Psych I so when I saw that one side of his face was entirely different than the other side, I started to ask M questions.

"No," she said, "I don't think he was particularly odd." But then she told me how he'd boil coins and tell his children that wildcats could eat thunder, and if they lied to him, old man Cyril would come in the night and steal their shoes. (Shoes were a very limited commodity in the Little family.) M was brought up on fear, not only of Old Cyril, but fear that God was watching every move she made, listening to every word, and there were terrible punishments awaiting her after death (I guess that's why she took everyone's death so hard). Fear that if she opened her mouth too much, no man would want her. Fear that if she didn't do what she was told, she'd be cast out into the cold. Fear that if she didn't eat every morsel on her plate, she'd have to sit at the table until she did, even when it turned moldy and bugs crawled in it. (This was true.) She tried to rein me in with some of these stories, but it never worked—only in the case of not going into Curtsey's Candy store. I knew she was telling the truth about Curtsey because Ginnie told me he'd stuck his dirty old man hand with long fingernails up her skirt one day when she went in for a pack of Teaberry gum.

~

My other grandparents were more recent immigrants. In fact my dad, though born here, had gone back and lived in the Isle of Man for a while when he was a kid. Margaret and Nigel Quayle (my dad's folks) were Manx, though there was probably a Viking or two mixed in the gene pool. Everyone had red hair and the Vikings were the only ones in history to conquer and hold the tiny island in the Irish Sea (for 400 years). Since there was no work for Nigel on the Isle of Man, he went to Africa to work in the diamond mines. There must have been some stories there, but I was never to hear them as he was dead long before I was born and no one bothered to remember or retell them. He did two three-year stints after they were married while Grandma Q stayed in Peel with her baby (Uncle Ernest). Finally they decided that they couldn't stand being apart any longer. One would hope that they chose America over South Africa because they disagreed with the political situation, the discrimination and mistreatment of black Africans. They had friends of all races in this country, but Grandma Q once said she hadn't wanted to live among Heathens!

This was a very bad decision on her part as they ended up in Cecily, Pennsylvania and Grandpa worked in the coal mines until black lung took him, not an easy death. I'm not even sure if he was around long enough to meet my mother. All I know about him is that he spoke three languages: English, Chinese, and an African dialect that no one recognized and was useless here. He was the guy who detonated dynamite in the mines which sounds like a good job, but apparently didn't pay very well as my dad had to work from the time he was twelve and they ate a lot of potatoes and stew, poor people's food.

In the old photos of them he's shorter than grandma Q and appears "quite jolly." He looked more like a disheveled professor than an adventurer who'd lived in Africa and it's possible that he never combed his hair, not for pictures anyway. To this day, I can't resist a man with wild hair.

~

Whereas Gram Little was a small sturdy farm woman who spoke with a mild crackly voice, Grandma Q was tall, imposing.She spoke in a piercing soprano with what sounded to us like an English accent. Though she was poor up until she married George Skifflington when she was 69 years old, she was charismatic and impossible to ignore. It's a good thing she didn't use fear to influence people like the Littles did, or we'd all be cringing in corners to this day.

When she spoke, people listened. She believed that as long as you gave respect to the "little folk" (fairies, elves, buggane, phynnodderee, and such), things would go reasonably in your favor, and if not, "buck up and muddle through." A philosophy much more to my own liking than that of the Littles (and a bit heathen, don't you think?).

~

With Uncle Walter gone, the family lost track of Aunt Anne for years until she turned up again and married Uncle Howdy after Aunt Betty died. Where she'd been and how she happened to turn up at this time, no one seemed to know. A curious coincidence, but it was the custom for grown-ups not to talk about certain things in front of children in those days.

I LOVED Aunt Betty; she didn't die until I was away in college so I missed that funeral. Aunt Betty drank a case of Coca Cola every day of her life until she was forty-nine years old and would let you drink as much Coke as you liked and do whatever you wanted in her house. "You brought paints!

Oh, great lets spread them out on the living room floor." "You learned how to build a campfire in Girl Scouts. You can burn the trash for me; here's matches." She was always laughing her head off at nothing and she wore things like flowered capris and visors, stuff M wouldn't be caught dead in.

When she was forty-nine, the doctor told her to give up Coca Cola for health reasons so she substituted ice tea in similar amounts. When I think now of all the caffeine and sugar she consumed, I guess it was drink that killed her too.

~

Another uncle died within two years of Uncle Walter.

Uncle Alfred was M's little brother. It was a big shock to everyone. Fine one day, then heart attack, wham! Uncle Alfred had three jobs and six kids. (You don't need invisible friends when you have brothers and sisters, though some kids have them anyway.) The oldest was a year and a half older than me; the youngest was two. His wife, Aunt Bonny, was in a continual caffeine/nicotine trance. As far as I know, she'd always been in the some kind of synaptic haze. Every time we were at their house, Uncle Alfred was out working and she was sitting at the kitchen table drinking coffee, smoking cigarettes and folding laundry. She was beautiful in a white-trash kind of way, patient and quiet despite her affinity for stimulants, only her teeth were horsy. She stayed in her daze when Alfred died, even though everyone else lost it. They really lost it.

I was taken to this funeral and wished I hadn't been, no one was protected from the chaos and hysteria. Uncle Alfred was a Divine Kingdom Apostle, as was Gram Little. The Apostles didn't have preachers; anyone that wanted to, got up and "testified." People stood in front of the room and screamed, cried, carried on until they were dragged off and someone else took their place. It was brutal. It went on all afternoon and into the evening until Mr. Wojtonowski threatened to throw them out. You couldn't understand a word they said; all the kids were scared, even the teenagers. Gram was in her glory with all the attention her son had attracted. She wasn't angry that everyone was out of control.

I understand why Aunt Bonny stayed in a daze that day.

I don't think I went to the cemetery because I'm sure I'd remember that. I wouldn't be surprised if an Apostle, or a few Apostles, didn't throw themselves into the grave; that's the kind of crowd it was. I never ever spoke to any of their kids about it or to any of the cousins; none of us dared mention it for fear it would set the grown-ups off again. What would I have said to them anyway? Gram told me the Divine Kingdom Apostles believe that at the end of the world a (rocket?) ship will take 111,326 sinless people to heaven, only 111,326 people out of the whole history of the world. What chance do you have? You're better off being Catholic, at least you can get forgiven in the end and Catholic Heaven is big enough to hold a lot more people—then again you could end up in Catholic Purgatory, which really sucks. Protestants don't have Purgatory and Jews don't like to talk about the afterlife at all. I like the Jain idea of afterlife; when their souls are finished reincarnating, they float to the dome of the universe. The idea of a dome full of floating souls appeals to me, a spiritual fish tank that never smells or has to be cleaned out. I always liked swimming.

I don't officially belong to any of these, not even to the High Anglican of my Manx grandparents. I have my own beliefs, my own rituals. I've made up my own religion, sort of like L. Ron Hubbard, only without any other followers. I don't encourage followers and I don't proselytize. Once you get to know me, you'll get the picture.

Some of the other cousins stayed in touch with Aunt Bonny and her kids, but I don't really know what happened to them. I heard that most of them moved down south and Aunt Bonny was still alive a few years ago—so much for caffeine and nicotine health concerns. You do have to be a certain kind of person to survive; there's a mutant body chemistry that thrives on these drugs. It definitely came through Aunt Bonny's side because M's family was pretty good customers of Mr. Wojtonowski and others, as you'll see—all except Gram, who lived to be 110, but that comes later.

~

There was a lull in family deaths for a few years. I continued to stage elaborate funerals for small animals and broken toys, but I plotted a boycott of "people funerals" after the Uncle Alfred fiasco.

One of my elaborate celebrations was held for a stuffed Panda bear, Mr. Presley—named after Elvis, of course. Mr. P was the size of a four-year-old child and was given to me by Uncle Ernest, my dad's only sibling. He and my dad were nothing alike; they didn't even look alike. Uncle Ernest was a gambling man, he gambled on anything, taught me to read racing forms. (Pop almost killed him for that.) Uncle E presented me with many fine gifts when he was on winning streaks; he won Mr. Presley on a punchboard game.

I considered myself much too old for stuffed animals at the time; I was in the fourth grade after all! But I loved Uncle E and didn't want to seem ungrateful. I was not an admirer of "girly" things either, pink rooms and collections of dolls and stuffed animals. I'd outgrown my asthma and had a bike, a black English Racer which my dad paid $15 for (used) at Mr. Kooser's Swap Store. I named it "Silent Beauty." I thought of myself as an adventurer, after all I was the descendant of a man who lived in Africa and probably knew Tarzan and pygmies and tribal chiefs; I was descended from Vikings and Seneca Indians. I was going to see the world some day, or at least Pittsburgh. And if some kids laughed at me, Mr. Rogers always liked me just the way I was—and so did Uncle E.

I was even beyond playing doctor; I played surgeon. At least once a week I put a sign on my bedroom door, "Operation in Progress." The first time I cut into Mr. P, I inserted a heart. Later I added various other trinkets: pennies, magazine pictures, buttons, cards and pieces of candy, in lieu of organs—Munchausen's disease by Stuffed Panda Proxy. Mr. P had a fine collection of scars. When he finally succumbed, all the neighborhood kids turned out for the funeral, kids who ranged in age from five to eleven. There was a grand parade, New Orleans style, with decorated bikes and umbrellas, kazoo and drum music, Paula on her clarinet, everyone in fancy outfits (and a few Halloween costumes), and readings from various favorite books including *Danny Dunn and the Anti-Gravity Paint*, *David and the Phoenix*, and original poetry by yours truly. Amen.

Afterward there was a mourning period of one week, when no one was allowed to mention Elvis Presley (the man) or listen to his records. It was agony.

The real Elvis Presley may have had more mourners, but his funeral wasn't any more elaborate (OK, maybe a little). The big difference was that there were no sightings of the panda Presley after his demise. Apparently inanimate things do not have ghosts or reincarnations; when they're gone, they're gone—except in movies.

~

This is unlike other characters who've been categorized (unfairly) as "unreal." Take for instance, the Lone Ranger.

My first acquaintance with The Ranger was over the radio. How old was I? It was before TV, or at least TV in our house, so I was four, five, six?

"Who was that masked man?" For many of us (for me anyway), it was our first experience of loss. He was there, he saved someone, and then…gone. "Who was that masked man?" You have to admit, that is the ultimate question. Being, Not Being, who cares what it's all about? Maybe we're better off not knowing anyway. But who is the masked man? Who will save us? Who will bring justice? And doesn't everyone want to inspire a faithful Indian companion? I wanted to **be** that faithful Indian companion. I knew I was uniquely suited to the role. I just had to find the elusive masked man who was out there saving people, getting the bad guy and doing good in the world. I discovered that there were lots of people out there wearing masks, but they were not The masked man.

Actually, the Lone Ranger did accompany me for years. Invisible? Yes, but when I screamed that we'd left him behind, my dad would always open the car door, even in the pouring rain. In dreams when I needed saving, the Ranger would appear. And you know he lives on. Even though the world today is much too complicated for one man (and an Indian companion) to save, his energy lives on and he appears occasionally (maybe in an alternate form) to get the bad guy.

Look for the white hat.

You can believe in whatever you want, but for me it's the Lone Ranger. He never said he could save the world, just a person here and there if he was in the neighborhood.

~

We were only fourth graders, for God's sake! What did we know about death? In the whole class only two other kids remembered a dead relative, Eugene his grandmother, and Alva Perry who had an aunt who drank herself to death. This is what Alva's mother told her; Alva never saw the body. For some reason we imagined Alva's aunt would be enormous, a giant water balloon of a person. Mikey Morse once drank four cartons of chocolate milk at lunch and it didn't kill him though he did throw up in gym class. We wondered why Alva Perry's aunt didn't just throw up her chocolate milk or what ever it was she drank. And we wondered why she would drink so much. Mikey Morse was an idiot and a show-off.

Shouldn't grown-ups know better?

I didn't want to be reminded of my two dead uncles, all waxy and made-up. I knew that what you saw in the boxes didn't look much like the "alive people" you'd known. I remembered getting reprimanded for being too noisy and having to go inside and sit by the dead body in the hushed presence of grown-ups until I sneezed so much from the flowers that they sent me out again. It was always cold in funeral parlors. Some grown-ups went outside to smoke cigarettes but they didn't pay much attention to us kids. Only Aunt Francis, who smoked a lot, asked us about school and what we were going to do in the summer and brought out cookies and Cokes so we didn't have to go inside and use our manners.

Some of the kids were afraid of dead bodies and when Tessa's dad died, they didn't want to go. But everybody liked Tessa and felt sorry for her. When I told them how all my relatives, even those from Missouri and Florida, came to see the uncles when they died, and we had to keep the uncles in boxes for a whole week before they could put them in the ground, and my mother said it was such a comfort for the living to have them there…they were convinced it would be right for us to go, the grown-up thing to do.

In our town, nobody got worried if you didn't go home right after school. They figured you went to a friend's or were playing ball or jumping rope in the schoolyard. Most of the parents were working at the mill or sleeping for the next shift or watching soap operas on TV.

The funeral home was on the hill, the biggest house in town, about a mile from our school. Alva and Bonny picked flowers on the way there. Mikey Morse cursed us out and we told him he didn't have to come but he said he didn't want to miss a dead body and came anyway. I told everybody about my dead uncles and how my cousins had to go live with the swamp people in Florida and we never saw them again. I hoped that wouldn't happen to Tessa; she had a pogo stick she let us use, and knew more jump-rope chants than anyone. I told them what my cousin BobbyRay told me, that they drain the blood out and fill them full of antifreeze so they won't rot, like the Egyptians did with their mummies. Peggy, whose dad was the town doctor, said she'd seen an Egyptian once when they went to her dad's college reunion. Everyone was impressed and I thought seeing a real Egyptian was every bit as good as seeing a dead body.

The woman at the funeral home looked a little surprised to see fourteen fourth graders (Marsha Kasiewicz had the flu and Tessa was presumably already there). The lady took the flowers from Alva and Bonny and led us into a dark room that smelled funny and had a lot of sad people. I didn't see Tessa. We stood close together and everyone looked at us. Finally, a lady said, "Go on up, children" and we moved forward, toward the box.

Inside was a skeleton of a thing in a sort of a blue nightgown with a blanket tucked up to the waist and long grey hair. Long hair and shrunken, but unmistakable, boobs!

Bonny started to cry and Mikey Morse laughed. Some of the other boys laughed too and Alva hit Billy Yoder who was laughing so hard he snorted. The funeral lady came running in and chased us out. We ran.

"What do you think you're doing," she screamed at us when we got to the door.

"We came to see Mr. Lombardi," I said. Four of the girls were crying and five of the boys ran out. "We're Tessa's friends."

"Oh," she said. "Mr. Lombardi. He's in the blue room but you can't go in there and carry on like this."

Bonny, Alva and two other girls left. The rest of us got ourselves together and went to the blue room but we never went up to see Tessa's dad because Tessa looked so embarrassed when she saw us, we didn't want her to feel worse. I guess she was ashamed that her father had gotten sick and died on her. Some of us tried to tell her we were sorry but she just put her head down and didn't answer. There were no cookies so after a few minutes we shuffled out and went home.

We never did hear who was laid out in the other room, even Tessa didn't know. We did have a lot of laughs over it, the look on the funeral lady's face, Loretta Fidazzo tripping on the carpet when we ran out, the flowers we knocked over... When Tessa came back to school she was very serious and sad until we told her the story, and then she started to laugh and she turned back into the old Tessa.

~

Another father died when we were in junior high. The girl was out of school for a couple of weeks to sit *Shiva*. There were very few Jews in our town and because I was her friend and I had a reputation for knowing about "strange" customs, the other kids asked me questions. "Why didn't they have a wake?" "They don't allow Jews to be buried in our cemetery, do they?" "Is it true they bury Jews upside-down? "

You must remember this was Bible Belt country; there were only two Jewish families in the town, which had been formed in an isolated valley in northern Appalachia that was really nowhere. We were north of the South and south of the North. Nowhere. Our teachers had been trained, minimally, in local Teachers Colleges. Most people had never even been to Pittsburgh which was forty miles away. A few miles south of Smiggle's, in West Virginia, they had better schools and hospitals, but we were in the forgotten part of Pennsylvania. The unions (that had done great things in the early days) took everyone's money and fled; the mines were being closed, the mills were going down too. There was no other industry popping up and the rest of the state, and the rest of the country just didn't care. Folks get some weird ideas when they're left alone in the mountains.

Strange questions buzzed around again when my friend's mother married her dead husband's brother several years later.

There's a passage in the bible that says that a man's brother must marry his widow. It doesn't take into account the fact that there might be only one other Jewish man in a hundred mile radius, that time passes and two lonely people get used to supporting each other, that they're not necessarily following an ancient law but following their hearts.

# Chapter 2

## A Short History of My Town

(How my parents ended up there was because Pop got a job with the electric company when he got out of the Navy.)

Sometime in the 1780s, Colonel Zachariah Ordwald Smigelski got it into his head that he could find a passage through the Appalachian Mountains into French Territory in order to escape prosecution for a minor infraction having to do with a Puritan deacon from the New England colonies. (The infraction was never specified. It was probably nothing compared to what goes on today. Then again, Smigelski trudged pretty far into the wilderness in order to get away...) Colonel Smigelski, not being the most accomplished of navigators, got lost in the hills and realized that he had no head for heights when random views triggered dizziness, nausea, and further disorientation. After suffering what seemed an overlong march, he staggered downhill and gave up in our valley when he saw he could get water from the Youghiogheny River. "Good enough," he pronounced and sat himself down, never to run again. Hence the name, Smigelski's Bottom, which was changed to Smiggle's Bottom to make it easier to spell. (You'd have to spend some time there to understand and you don't really want to do that.) Though the people there are "river-folk" and were undoubtedly much smaller in size than folks today, the town was founded ninety years before Tolkien was born, so the name has nothing to do with the Gollum character in his books (which is pronounced and spelled differently, but some outsiders ask about it anyway).

Emigrants and travelers began to stop a few miles upriver to build rafts on which to float down the Yough. Occasionally, a raft built by a less competent traveler, crashed or fell apart near Smiggle's and they were encouraged to give up their dream and settle in a place that at least had water, timber, and a stone quarry. When coal was discovered under Smiggle's Bottom, it was the descendants of some of these people who died young in the "patches," or became wealthy beyond all comprehension and left the town for a more august existence.

Yes, there were rich people at one time, a few who ran the coal and coke industries. Railroads and riverboats carried great loads to the mills in Pittsburgh. But the coal was pretty much mined out by the 1960s and it had become more economical to dig in other states or import coal from other countries. In the early days, the unions fought hard for equitable pay and better working conditions, but when things started looking bad and they had collected all the money they could from their members, they absconded, leaving the place dangerously undermined—scarred by strip mines, slag heaps, and crumbling coke ovens. Abandoned mines caved in, pulling houses and roads down with them; sending noxious gasses into the air above. Generations went on Relief with no hope of ever getting away.

The unions took over some of the mansions that were left behind, renovated them (importing workmen and materials from other places and countries), and used them as retreats for their officials.

The town died. Can you feel it?

~

When I was very young, we had a movie theater in town, but it became a Revival Center about the time I turned eleven. I wasn't much interested in being saved in the religious sense; I didn't see how it did anyone much good. What I wanted to be saved from was Smiggle's Bottom. Had they offered me a trip to Disney World, I would have signed up in a heartbeat; Cleveland or even

McKeesport would have done it. What my soul needed was adventure, intrigue, the Lone Ranger...

In terms of entertainment, there were two drive-ins that were reasonably close and, in the winter, there were ponds to skate on. There were woods and the river...there weren't many live fish to be had and you had to be pretty desperate to eat one because the mines and the mills had dumped a lot of gunk in the Yough through the years. (But we had no problem swimming in it.) Hunting season was the high point of the year. They closed the high school on the first day of hunting season because none of the boys showed up and, therefore, few girls bothered to come (girls didn't much count anyway).

Men, and some women, dressed in festive orange regalia. They tip-toed through the woods and occasionally shot one another by accident.

Dead deer arrived strapped to cars in a triumphant parade. Pheasant and rabbit carcasses were prominently displayed. The kills were hung in back yards, measured, weighed, showed off, and compared. Then they were stripped of their skin, gutted, and eaten. Antlers were preserved as hat racks and back scratchers. Guns were ceremoniously cleaned and put away, but not far away.

Many of the people living in Smiggle's had food names: Bean, Fish, Mellon, Troutman, Buttermore, Livermore, MacIntosh, Pancake, Lamb, Plum, Berry. They named their children Ginger, Stewart, Cherry, Olive, Pepper, Candy, Hazel. Waitresses always called you Hon (or Honey); children and lovers had pet names like Pumpkin, Muffin, Dumpling. Or your nickname might be Peanut, Rabbit, Cheesy. If you were disliked, you might end up as Toast. If you were something less than crazy, you were Squirrelly. Don't get me started on names—there were some doozies.

The valley made everyone a little crazy or a little desperate. Girls started getting pregnant in the eighth grade; food and sex, what else was there to do?

~

After the initial birth-shock which I'll tell you about later, I was pretty happy in Smiggle's Bottom up until puberty. We had secret clubs and hideouts; we jumped off railroad bridges into the river to swim; we walked into town to ride the only elevator, in Sproat's Department Store—four floors! Then puberty happened.

The girls got interested in boys and sex. A lot of them tried to get pregnant because husbands came with babies in those days. It might have been a little embarrassing at first, but you got to quit school (you **had** to quit school) and could even contrive a way to move out of your parents' house.

I wanted to get out of town, so I aspired to a career rather than a husband. I wasn't interested in getting pregnant. I could indulge my sexual fantasies all by myself, thank you. I'm eternally grateful for Whitie's Store and his inventory of *MAD Magazine*, weird comics, and paperbacks. Thank goodness for Patti Rush, Paula Rock, Bert, and Smidtke. Thank goodness for Celery Morris, Jerry, Marty, and Rockwell. Thank goodness for Mr. Lieb who had the compassion to pass me in algebra even though I didn't understand a thing; Miss Thompson, J. Fredric Hunter, and Miss Roland, the good teachers I had there. Thank goodness M and Pop saved up from the day I was born to send me to a big-time college like West Virginia University.

Thank goodness I was blessed with a splendid inner life— and other lives to occupy myself with.

"all good things must come to an end"

# Chapter 3

## Secrets and Not-So-Secret Stuff

This is the part about my last life. You may not want to read about it if you don't believe in that kind of stuff. Or you may want to collect data from firsthand experience. I've never put this out for public consumption before and I purposefully put it in the context of fiction and maybe it is. You can take it anyway you like. I don't care.

Just before you fall asleep, you drift into a state scientists call a "hypergolic state;" you're not quite asleep and not quite awake. In this state, I would occasionally have a vision, a vision of something so frightening and so real that it woke me up, sweating and shaking. I was so terrified that I couldn't go back to sleep and I couldn't remember what it was I'd seen.

This took place once every few months, ever since I could remember—and earlier! It began before I could put it into words.

When I was in high school, I had a wonderful English teacher named Miss Roland who gave us what she called "browsing lists." These were books that she put on reserve in the library for us to "browse through." The subject and books changed every couple of months and we had to write a report on our "browsings."

The unit on "Oriental Philosophy" fascinated me. Many of the concepts matched my own feelings about life, but I never dreamed that such ideas existed in anyone else's head, much less in a whole culture. I didn't think it would be possible to live in the modern Western world in the manner of monks in China and Tibet, and I knew it was totally improbable in Smiggle's Bottom, but I was captivated by their ideas. I was especially attracted to a book by Lin Yu Tang (I think that was his name). I interpreted one passage to mean that you had to stand up and face your "dragon," allow yourself to be consumed by it and you would come out unscathed.

Whether this is exactly what he said or meant, I don't know. I was young and that's what I got from it. Miss Roland didn't disagree. I took the passage to heart and decided I would train myself to stand up to my hypergolic "vision," to face it and stay with it long enough to remember what it was that frightened me so much. Every night I chanted my intention with teenage conviction and urgency, "I will not be afraid. I will stay and remember." "I will not be afraid. I will stay and remember."

The vision didn't appear every night. Sometimes, it was months between occurrences. Each time it happened, I'd freeze in fear and wake up unable to remember, despite my determination.

It took years.

Sometime before I went away to college, I was finally successful. In my hypergolic state, I stood on the unsteady lip of a cliff, overlooking a huge abyss. I was petrified; I was dizzy; I was about to go over the edge. I knew the fall was extensive, terrifying, and painful but I stayed long enough to remember…I faced my "dragon." I'd always been afraid of heights, and still am, but I haven't had the "vision" since that night.

I knew, even then, that it was more than a "vision." It was too real; it had to be a memory. I wracked my brain for a place I'd been that matched it, but there was no such place. I asked my parents if they'd taken me anywhere like that as a baby or young child and they said "no." I didn't tell them why I was asking since they didn't think I had a clear understanding of the difference between real and unreal—and maybe I don't. (More on this later.) I didn't tell anyone about this for a long time. I knew that I had gone over this cliff, and not of my own volition.

It took me years to understand that it was a vision of a violent death in another life. It took many more years to tell anyone. It's not that I don't want to admit that we have other lives; this, I think, is a good thing. It's that I'd been laughed at or worse, treated like I was crazy at times in my life and I didn't want to encourage this attitude. I didn't want to be noticed. And I didn't think my life, or my previous lives, were anyone else's business.

~

EVERYBODY DESERVES TO HAVE A SECRET. IF YOU DON'T HAVE ONE, GO OUT AND GET ONE RIGHT AWAY. DON'T HURT ANYONE AND DON'T DO ANYTHING YOU'LL HAVE TO FEEL GUILTY OR BAD ABOUT TO GET ONE. BUT GET ONE!

~

This brings me to a story that isn't about Toad Omalacy, but does happen in his yard. I was probably about seven at the time and we lived in the Fourgoose house. It was a huge old house divided in two. It looked like the Bates' house in *Psycho* or the Addams family home. The Fourgoose family lived in the other side of the house, but we used the same staircase to get upstairs to the bedrooms. My father got up at 5:00 a.m. in the winter to shovel coal into the furnace so it would be warm when everyone else got up. When people came to visit, they thought "Sherman Fourgoose" on the mailbox was a joke. It was no joke that Freddie Fourgoose (who was a year older than me) beat me up once, for no good reason, and chipped my tooth.

A lot of strange things happened in the Fourgoose house.

I was sick for three months in the second grade and no one could figure out what was wrong with me. In those days, you didn't go to the hospital, unless it was an asthma attack and you couldn't breathe. The doctor came to you. (You shouldn't go to a hospital now unless you really have to.) First, he said I had scarlet fever (or was it rheumatic fever—what color is that?) Then it was chicken pox & measles at the same time. All I remember is fire, heat and fire, and that I wasn't allowed to walk. My dad had to carry me upstairs to bed at  night and down in the morning so M could take care of me while she did her housework. Freddie Fourgoose thought all this was a hoot but I didn't notice at the time as I was sheathed in a shroud of fever fire.

There was a pear tree in the yard that made eerie shadows on my bedroom wall and a convent (that we called a "nunnery") across the street—though we rarely saw any nuns. The Fourgoose house and the street it was on was so decrepit that the whole neighborhood was razed a few years after we moved out. They were supposed to build a strip mall on the site, but it never got past a few cinderblock walls for years. I think there's something there now though, a junk yard or a garage.

I was the only girl on the block and there was Toad Omalacy, Freddie Fourgoose, Sonny Koontz, and Booger Benzio, who were my age. Toad was my best friend though, because he was too fat to run very much and I had asthma and couldn't run.

Toad's yard had some scraggily bushes that passed as hedges around it and we used to play in them, making roadways for little cars and trucks. One day, we were playing in the bushes and Toad had to go to the bathroom so he went into the house. I was busy playing for a while when I realized he'd been gone a long time. I looked up toward the backdoor hoping to see him come out, and there in Toad Omalacy's mother's garden was a tiger! A tiger! Nibbling at Mrs. Omalacy's vegetables!

I'd watched enough TV by that time to know that if that tiger hadn't noticed me, I must be downwind. I remember thinking "downwind" and praying that the wind wouldn't change because it looked like he was hungry and I didn't think tigers normally subsisted on backyard lettuce and tomato plants. I backed out of the bushes quietly, down the hill behind Toad's house, and started running. I didn't wait for the Lone Ranger. When I got home, I was soaked in fear-sweat and shaking so hard that my mother couldn't peel my wet clothes off me. She tried to calm me down by telling me it must have been the Hardy's bird dog, but I knew a dog from a tiger when I was seven. Who was she kidding?

Here was my very own mother telling me that I couldn't tell real from unreal. I'd heard it before and would hear it all my life. Shy to begin with, after this event I was afraid to open my mouth; I couldn't trust myself to discern reality and I didn't want to wind up in the "loony bin." I made a conscious decision to stay quiet, watch what others did and said, and try to be invisible.

It was years before I learned that other people don't know real from unreal either and just didn't admit to it. Hell, most of them don't even know how crazy they are!

~

In terms of Afterlife, this raises the possibility of eternal bullshit.

~

We moved out of the Fourgoose house when I was eight and I never heard from any of those kids again; South Smiggle had its own grade school and everyone moved out when they tore the neighborhood down. So, by high school, they were all gone. When I was in my twenties, my mother told me she heard that Toad Omalacy had shot himself. This is very sad and has to do with having an older brother who does everything better and is better looking. I'm sorry I called Toad fat. He really wasn't; it's just that he hadn't had his requisite growth spurt yet. He was fun and funny and had hair like a Golden Retriever, soft and yellow. What could have been so bad? Look around.

I'm sorry that he didn't get to see the tiger, or ride in an airplane, or hear The Beatles, or see the Seinfeld show on TV. Hell, he may not have even gotten to eat Chinese food because it didn't arrive in Smiggle's Bottom until the Mall, which was long after I'd left.

~

Our high school prom queen shot herself also, but she'd tried a lot of other ways to kill herself before settling on the gun.

see p.

She taught me how to hide pimples with Calamine Lotion and suggested I wear a padded bra (I did in high school). It's seldom that a popular girl is so nice to a person like me. You'd wonder what could be so bad if boys like you and your pimples never showed. The truth was that her mother had a violent boyfriend and six or seven other (younger) kids. When things got rough at her mother's house, she'd take a sister or two and walk across town to her grandmother's to stay for a few days. Her grandmother was really strict so that wasn't much fun either. When things got really bad, she'd swallow a handful of pills and end up getting her stomach pumped. (This is what she was doing the night of the prom she was supposed to be crowned queen of.)

It seems to me that if you had thoughts of killing someone in such a situation, you'd murder your mother's boyfriend, not yourself.

~

When I was in my thirties and living in New York, I knew a woman who set herself on fire. She had a couple of kids and was a big admirer of Georgia O'Keefe. (Flowers that look like female private parts on steroids—I never understood the attraction.) Burning is a painful way to go. Not recommended.

A very famous and talented man put a plastic bag over his head. What was he thinking?

I could go on and on about this, but the truth is: there are easier ways. And if you're going to do it, you should really be suffering—from some incurable disease or terrible physical mutation that keeps you from having a life. Something irrevocable. My feeling is, you can always start over. Why not? Dump everything and go somewhere else, be a different person.

33

Maybe you can be a different person right where you are, or the same person somewhere else where it would be more comfortable. There are many options.

If not, take pills. Breathe in gas only if you're sure you won't be found because it causes brain damage if you live—which might take care of your problems anyway, or make them worse. Think hard before you do something like this.

When I was a teenager and got depressed, I wrote long agonized suicide notes (with no intention of actually doing It). I wrote them to famous people, people I saw on the street, people I didn't know. Putting self-pity down on paper is a hoot. You end up laughing yourself right out of your mood. I recommend it.

THE ALTERNATIVE TO DYING IS GETTING OLD. SOME PEOPLE DO THIS REALLY WELL; THEY'RE WISE AND HAPPY AND FUN TO BE AROUND. OTHERS ARE A PAIN; THEY GET GROUCHY AND MEAN AND DEMANDING—THEY WERE UNDOUBTEDLY LIKE THAT WHEN THEY WERE YOUNG BUT THEY GOT WORSE. UNFORTUNATELY, WE DON'T ALL BECOME WISE WITH AGE. STICK WITH THE ONES IN THE FIRST GROUP. IF YOU'RE STUCK WITH SOMEONE IN THE GROUCHY CATEGORY, I FEEL SORRY FOR YOU BUT DON'T DESPAIR; YOU DON'T HAVE TO TURN INTO THEM EVEN IF THEY ARE YOUR FATHER.

~

In terms of people who are fun to be around (at least for outsiders), I think of Ernie Kovacs.

There are people we relate to and people we don't relate to, despite blood or propinquity. I totally related to Ernie Kovacs when I was a kid. He put on TV what was going on in my head:

liquids that poured sideways, monkey bands, whole rooms that turned on their side or upside down, "intellectuals" who made no sense whatsoever. I never missed his show. I wrote asking if I could come visit him and Edie, and burned the letters in a friend's fireplace hoping the smoke would reach him and lead him to find me, as we were kindred spirits. I believed this sort of ritual was something akin to what my Seneca ancestor might perform.

I was sixteen when he died in a car accident. My dad used to get the Pittsburgh Press on Sundays, or maybe it was on the TV news—probably both. There was a picture of him, his head hanging out of an open car door, blood dripping out of his ear into a puddle on the ground. I can still see it now and will remember that picture forever. I never got to meet him but I felt the loss. It was the first hole in the world that I experienced personally, the first one that would never be plugged up—for me. Isn't it strange how someone you don't really know can mean so much? And how the loss of an actual blood-uncle barely makes a dent.

I don't know what happened to Edie, but I think she ultimately remarried and had a new life. I hope she didn't see that picture.

~

Here's what I miss about my hometown: swimming in the river, chocolate shorts (a drink, like egg creams), graham cracker milkshakes, Annie Oakley (a local "crazy" who walked around with toy guns strapped to her waist), Silent Beauty (my bike), walking on railroad tracks, drive-in movies, real spring water, Wolfman McFern, Whitie's, and Kooser's General Store.

Not many of these things are still there.

~

# Chapter 4

## Calling(out) Names

Here's how I got my name: my parents, the ever-proper AJ and Rose Quayle, chose what they thought was a very auspicious name for their child, a child that they'd waited and prayed seven years for, a child Rose Quayle nearly died for and had to deliver Cesarean because we both had toxemia.

*My mother made a deal with God (or someone) to let her and her baby have a life. She died on my forty-sixth birthday, when her contract was up. I don't know when mine is up.*

This is not a story about a child who was neglected or abused, like most stories you read today. This is a story about a much loved and cared for child, an "only" child who came late in life, a miracle child. That is, it was a miracle that I got here, not that I'm capable of performing miracles or anything more astounding than bending the top knuckle of my index finger while keeping the rest of the finger straight—which is a pretty good trick that not many people can do.

I'm not going to tell you the name they chose for me as I'm superstitious about strangers, even acquaintances and friends, knowing my real name. I don't want to think that there's a reason anyone would want to curse me, but you never can tell.

They chose a name that had a tone of virtuous Biblical piety, as well as the promising energy of a beloved friend, a name they gave grave consideration to. However, I came into the world railing against fate and label.

There's a Zen saying that "A snowflake never falls in the wrong place." Don't believe it. Not that I didn't appreciate Rose and AJ, they were kind and loving, as well-meaning as anyone in this world. But being buried in that nowhere valley, undermined by abandoned coal shafts that were routinely caving in and oozing gases; surrounded by slag heaps and old coke ovens (which people actually lived in)…Well, it might be OK when you're little and don't know any better, but once you hit puberty, you just want out.

I was a misfit from the beginning, not in a good way, not a Brando or James Dean way, not an Audrey Hepburn or Janis Joplin way. I was not supposed to be there, and I did NOT like my name. I wailed so continuously and distinctly that I became famous for my bawling. When anyone spoke my name, I let out a particularly deafening scream that set neighborhood dogs howling and gave adults headaches. I wasn't home from the hospital an hour when my Manx grandmother began calling me Felicity as a joke, but I approved. "Ah, that's more like it," I must have thought with my baby mind. And so I've been called Felicity all my life. Neither my enemies nor most of my friends know I have another name, and that's the way I like it.

Louis, my sainted husband (sainted because he puts up with a lot—more on that later), said I should change it legally because it's a problem on official papers. No chance. My life has gone quite well the way things are, why tempt cosmic forces. I rather like the addition of "AKA" on legal papers. I like it so well, I've added a couple other AKAs purely for their diversionary value (and my own amusement).

Louis is resigned to my quirks.

~

The funeral lull ended with a vengeance when I was in high school. Several cousins died. They were older than me but barely in their fifties. Drink took a few, a hereditary disease among the folks my mother's siblings chose to many. M's siblings seemed to be inordinately attracted to alcoholics. I understand why; young alcoholics can be engaging and seductive.

Take for instance Jim Morrison of the Doors. Not that any of my mother's siblings, or their children, married anyone as hot as Jim Morrison, though one cousin married a cop who looked like a young Elvis. Unfortunately, "Young Elvis," who might be a very nice guy but it's hard to tell because he never said a word, aged VERY badly. At sixty-two, he looked like a large worm-like farm animal or a camel that lost about a hundred pounds but was still overweight.

One cousin had a heart attack before he was fifty.

Most of the aunts and uncles on M's side chose strokes. Strokes are unpredictable; you can go fast or you can go slow. If you go slow, you might end up anywhere from slightly incapacitated to full-blown vegetable. None of my relatives saw it coming even though it became a family tradition. Whether or not you have a "life" afterward is a toss-up. Cousin Floyd was an intelligent, lively guy who ended up with the "quality of life" of a Brussels sprout. Aunt Lil was a maudlin lump who became a fury in a wheelchair. Go figure.

I did not attend any of these funerals. I convinced M that I'd been traumatized by Uncle Walter and Uncle Alfred's funerals when I was a child and pleaded important school activities. She said funerals were not an occasion to parade dead bodies around  frightened children, but to support survivors in their grief and that I should rethink my position. She let me off anyway.

I continued my funeral boycott for years.

V

~

In M's family, with few exceptions, only Gram got old. She resigned herself to watching everyone else die. At her one hundredth birthday, Aunt Flo read off the names and ages of Gram's children (nine) and grandchildren (forty-three), great grandchildren (six), and great greats (two). Four of her children and five of her grandchildren were dead, and Aunt Flo would die within the year. Gram never got angry after Uncle Walter's funeral; she laughed at herself when she forgot things, giggled when her parts didn't work right. She moved into a nursing home at ninety-nine, and became a celebrity. When they took a group to the circus or the Ice Capades, they'd introduce her: "We have in the audience today Mrs. Clara Little…" (her only husband had been dead for over fifty years and she still went by "Mrs.'") "…. she's 101 years old." "…she's 105 years old." "…she's 107 years old." Gram would stand up, wave and smile. People cheered. She ate it up.

When M called me in college to tell me Gram had died, I said, "I can't believe it." (She was 110 years old!) My mother said, "Your cousin Cora" (my very favorite cousin) "said, 'Are you sure?'" That kind of thing happens when someone gets to be that old; folks start to expect they'll live forever.

I didn't go to that funeral either, so I'll never be sure she's really dead. The attendants at the nursing home said they came in to change her bed one day and she sat down in a chair, heaved a sigh and "passed on" peacefully.

I don't much like the phrase "passed on," though we know that's exactly what it is, don't we? I always thought you should just say the person was "dead," since they wouldn't be around (in that form) anymore. "Dead" has a finality to it that doesn't give people the opportunity to question you. And people usually want to ask a lot of questions when someone dies: "How did it happen?" "When did it happen?" "Were you with them?" "Were they in pain?" "What's going to happen to that walnut end table they kept in the front room?"

What can you say? Whatever you do say, they have to respond to it and that's difficult. Some of the things people say to the bereaved are inane and embarrassing. The worst is, "Well, at least he's out of his misery." Out of his misery! He might have been uncomfortable, incapacitated in some way, but at least he was ALIVE. Now he's DEAD. That's a big jump. And that's supposed to make you feel better? I don't think so.

The truth of it is, other than the above stupidity, most anything that's said to you after someone close to you dies is comforting. If you don't tell any hurtful secrets about the dead person, you're in the clear. You can even tell funny stories or make jokes; these things ease the tension for a while and show that you remember.

~~

The main characters in this tale, a lot of the people in my life, are dead—with the exception of me and I have been, remember? Then again, by now everyone has probably been dead at least once, whether they remember it or not.

I come from hard-working farmers and mining stock. We may not all be sturdy, but we dig into the ground until we become a part of it. OK, I was not so grounded growing up. I was at risk of flying off the earth at any time and still must be wary of spontaneous levitation, though I've learned to think of it as a natural part of life and am resigned to surrendering to it periodically.

~

ACCORDING TO CHINESE ASTROLOGY, I'M A FIREDOG. MY CHILDHOOD WAS PUNCTUATED BY FEVER AND COAL. ASH FROM THE ALLEY BEHIND MY CHILDHOOD HOME, IS PERMANENTLY IMBEDDED IN ONE KNEE FROM AN OLD FALL. MY FATHER WORKED FOR THE ELECTRIC COMPANY. ONE DAY THESE PAGES WILL IGNITE AND THE REMAINS OF MY LIFE WILL BURN UP COMPLETELY.

~

You can't escape death. You certainly can't escape your own, and it's difficult to escape the death of others for long. My last escape was definitely not worth the trouble and has left me with a lot of guilt that I could have avoided.

Grandma Q had embraced her young widowhood for a long time. She was resigned to Tuesday pinochle, Thursday Bingo and a once a year Manx convention that she talked my dad into taking us to, three or four times. Grandma Q was quite a number, tall and dignified, even in her sixties and especially among the Manx ladies who were somewhat frumpy. To their credit, in the fifties when most women were either dowdy or tacky, the Manx ladies were frumpy in a European way that was exotically elegant next to

American women. The Manx ladies wore practical clothing and footwear, but favored whimsical hats.

Grandma Q met George Skifflington at a Manx convention in Cleveland. He was the only grandfather I ever knew and I loved him madly. He was always happy and called everyone "Mate." I was the flower girl at their wedding though the only guests were my parents, Uncle Ernest and me. When she moved to Miami with him, she asked what I wanted her to send me from there, a place no one I knew had ever been. I was nine and Miami was as good as Africa in terms of exotic. I thought it must be like Hawaii or Tahiti, places I'd read about in the library. I asked for a grass skirt.

And I got it.

Christmases we'd drive down to Florida to visit. It was two days of car-sickness and grumbling from my dad, then sunshine and all the shrimp you could eat. It seemed like everyone in Miami knew George Skifflington. He'd done fancy plastering for a living and worked on all the big hotels and churches, so he'd take us into these fancy places and managers would buy us drinks, priests would let us roam around during Christenings and weddings. My dad was embarrassed, but George Skifflington would just laugh, put his arm around Grandma Q and she'd giggle like a little girl. This would embarrass my dad even more.

There was a family that lived near them with a girl my age who had pierced ears and came to parrot jungle with us. Uncle Ernest went to dog races every day and met a woman, but he didn't marry her. Life in Miami was fast, fun, and full of parrots, flamingos, and pierced ears.

I was in college when George Skifflington died. I don't think my parents asked if I would go to that funeral; they'd given up on me going to funerals by then. I wouldn't have wanted to go;

Miami would never be the same without him. He left a big hole. Flamingos still make me sad.

Even though I was caught up in being away and the Sixties, I knew that something was happening to Grandma Q after he died. I hadn't gotten a package of Manx shortbread in a while and when I did, it was just crumbs and pieces of the plastic container she'd sent it in. Grandma Q was an accomplished packer; she sent packages to her relatives in the Isle of Man for fifty years, and I had never, ever seen a plastic container in her house. There was glass, ceramic, porcelain, but NEVER plastic. Grandma Q was not a plastic person. Her cookies had always come in sturdy cardboard and arrived intact.

I called my mother and told her to check on Grandma Q. Why didn't I call grandma myself? Long distance phone calls, in our family those days, were a rarity. They were only resorted to in times of crisis, extreme sickness, death. We wrote letters. I wrote letters home from college and I was only forty-five minutes away in West Virginia. (My dad would send them back with the misspelled words underlined in red pen. It was before computers and that's the kind of guy he was—and the kind of speller I still am.)

Within the month, Grandma Q had several strokes and was in the hospital. My parents called to say they would pick me up on the way down to Florida.

This was 1967 or '68 and people did fly in airplanes—but not Rose and AJ, not even when someone was dying. AJ would eventually take an airplane a few times. After Rose died, he would fly up to see me in New York. But they couldn't conceive of it back then. Grandma Q had flown to the Isle of Man three times. After she married George Skifflington, they went to visit once a year. At first they took the Queen Mary (or was it the Queen Elizabeth?), but after a few years, George convinced his bride they should save time and fly. It was a great event in our family. Grandma Q would always write long goodbye letters full of assertions of love and advice, as she was certain the plane would crash.

My parents picked me up in the midst of final week. My sad confession is that I would have rather stayed and taken my finals than drive down to Miami and watch my grandmother die.

The more I thought about watching her die, the sicker I got. The more I thought about seeing her in a casket and then never being able to remember her alive, like Uncle Walter, the more nauseous I got. By Maryland, I was throwing up out of the car window. It seems bizarre to me now, but my parents put me on a bus and sent me back to school. And I went gladly.

She died just after my folks got there. My dad sold the house and gave everything in it to the neighbors (he was not a materialistic sort of guy). This must upset Grandma Q no end. Ever since I can remember, she had little tags attached to the bottoms of her things with names of the people they were to go to when she died. I did get the frog vase with my name on it, thanks to my mother's quick thinking. I also got a pin that was made from great grandma Bull's "earbobs," which I take to be a pair of earrings that she had soldered together. My mother took a broach with small diamonds in it. Everything else disappeared.

~

My two dead grandmothers hovered about me for years. They crocheted and embroidered shadows while I attempted to get myself into trouble. They replaced the invisible friends of my youth but they were not there to entertain me.

On old TV shows, confusion was often represented by a tiny devil on one shoulder and an angel on the other shoulder of a character, telling him what to do. My Grandmothers took on this job: Grandma Little spouting Divine Kingdom Apostle ethics and fears, touting conservatism and restraint; Grandma Q encouraging me to take chances, see the world, look out for myself but have some fun—things she'd learned from George Skiffington. It's possible she might even have had regrets about not going to Africa when she had the chance, at least to see it once.

I should mention Rose Quayle (my mother)'s philosophy here. My mother had a simple technique to overcome depression. She just didn't think about herself. If you were bored staying home and your husband wouldn't let you work, don't think about it; offer to take someone who didn't drive, to the Mall; do the sick neighbor's laundry; help a friend paint her dining room. As easy as that.

Rose was a saint. As much as I'd like to, I can't honestly blame my mother for any of my faults. She did attempt to pass on an assortment of (baseless) fears, that she'd grown up believing. Over the years, she overcame many of them, though she never completely overcame the anxiety they imparted. They never much affected me and Grandma Q's advice to take chances won out over Grandma Little's fear-based warnings.

~

# Chapter 5

## Hearts and Spades

*"Ernie "Red"?"*

Then there was my pop.

Pop's shoes were always spit-shined, his clothes clean and pressed, never a stray crumb or stain on anything. Hands had to be washed every time you entered the house; pencils were lined up in the desk drawer with erasers all pointing in the same direction. Pop was home from his job at the electric company every weeknight by 5:30 p.m. He changed, read the paper, ate supper, and then spent a few hours practicing his magic tricks.

A magician's act and patter have to be well-rehearsed. Pop practiced (almost) every day of his life from the time he was twelve until his death at eighty-three. Each card in a new deck of cards was lightly coated with Elmer's Glue and powdered with Baby Powder. (This makes no sense to me now, but I saw him do it many times.)

Despite the obsessive neatness of our home, my parents allowed cards to remain stuck to the ceiling until they fell of their own accord. People loved to see my dad do tricks. For this particular trick, they chose a card, put it back in the deck without him seeing it and screamed in astonishment when he threw the deck up in the air and their card stuck to the ceiling. Such an exuberant display was very unlike my meticulously reserved father, but he was a different person when he performed. Not a trick he could do on stage or at a table in a restaurant where ceilings might be too high or uneven, this one was reserved for home.

My father's magic wand was broken symbolically and placed in his casket by fellow magicians, as is their custom. I tucked a deck of cards in his jacket where he could find them in the next world; they are cleaned and powdered, ready to fly through the air. His case of tricks rests on a high shelf in my closet and though I rarely open it, I know that amid the chaos of the world and the clutter and disorder of my life, there is still magic.

But I'm getting ahead of myself.

# Chapter 6

## The Sixties

Thank God someone did away with those irritating Fifties. Who was it? Martin Luther King? Mao? Kennedy? Elvis? Dylan? The Beatles? Dick Clark? Dr. Louis Leakey? Yuri Gagarin? Alan Shepard? Mohamed Ali?

The Fifties had a lot of outdated rules and we needed people to break them. We all helped, in our own way. What I liked most about the Fifties was the crinolines. I wasn't much for getting dressed up but when I did, I favored big swirly skirts with bright, crunchy crinolines beneath. I liked some of the music but most of it sucked. I liked polka dancing with old people at the Slovak Hall. I didn't like being made fun of for not having curves, and then the sixties hit and I was in style. Padded Bra? What bra? Who needed a bra?

*pedicoates*

And hair! What a great thing to hide behind. No more of M's "cute" haircuts. There was a time when my hair was longer than my skirt! There are pictures of me all legs and hair, a tall version of "Cousin It" from the Addams Family.

It was acceptable to be "spacey," a natural cognitive state for me. And to walk around in your bare feet, ahhhh. I was made for the sixties in many ways.

For me, they started the summer after my freshman year (1965), a little later than most but it was definitely still the fifties back in Smiggle's Bottom and there were still rebel flags over some fraternity houses at West Virginia University. I convinced my dad that I should go with a few friends to work on Cape Cod for the summer. Up there the sixties were in full swing and though I was never quite a "member in good standing" of any specific group, I was tolerated without mockery. (I was never good at fitting into a category and I did try at times.) People my age had become more liberal in the face of oddities, and in regard to the era of sixties "freaks," I was "normal."

My sexual fantasies, previously centered on TV and movie stars, expanded to rock stars. It's a good thing I was not in a position to become a groupie as I didn't have the best taste in (famous) men. I never understood the lure of Mick Jagger, but I was totally enamored of Keith Richards. Keith was the first guy to wear an earring. Keith didn't sing about "honky-tonk women" and then hang out with Lee Radziwill like Mick. Keith didn't pull any punches about his drug and alcohol use. Keith was always Keith—and still is, funny and surprisingly wise.

Of course, a girl as mousey as me would have no chance with someone who went out with wild and beautiful women like Anita Pallenberg, but what about Tim Buckley. He was dreamy, and isolated enough for me. Poor Tim, a casualty of the drug culture. Van Morrison? Nothing like an Irish crazy. I have a feeling that despite his talent, Van may not be the sort of person you'd want to wake up next to if he was in a dark mood. Though at the time, he seemed as if he might be kind of cuddly.

Dylan? Way too serious. We saw what he did to reporters and to poor Donovan in that movie (*Don't Look Back*) ...God forbid you should say something goofy around him. (And how could I help it?)

We don't really want to meet our idols in the flesh and sacrifice the fantasy we have of them, do we?

Ok, I have enormous respect for Dylan even though I'm intimidated by him. So, lighten up, Bob, and I'll take you out for ice cream.

It was good there were plenty of rock stars to fantasize about because our contemporary movie idols were not exactly sex symbols. Maybe DeNiro was for a minute (no, he was scary too). We were living the time of Dustin Hoffman, great actor, but not a turn-on. Al Pacino? His sex scenes are painful  to watch. I know it came later, but think of *Sea of Love*. Poor Ellen Barkin worked her tail off in those love scenes and Al...is he even human? Mickey Rourke is sexier, but talk about scary! John Malkovich is sexier but seems to have a dark side that you may not want to deal with. Peter Fonda? Dennis Hopper? Not into the "hipper than thou" boys. Sexy movie stars were from the older generation, not ours. It wasn't like today—there's a surplus of young hot actors, not to mention Johnny Depp.

Women of all ages are thankful for Johnny Depp.

And who was there to look up to in terms of female role models? Not the angry feminists; their bravery was admirable but God save us from intellectuals. Grace Slick? Too slick, too California. Janis. There was someone I could aspire to: wild, independent, gritty. I had the hair—if I didn't wash or brush it … but that was hard to do when you come from an obsessively neat household. I did my best.

And then Janis went...

Luckily, I lived too much in my own fantasies to totally succumb to the excesses of the period. I was always able to "stand on my own head," as my Manx grandmother used to say. It was a good thing because a lot of the people I admired "bit it" early on.

~

I call these people "relatives" for the purpose of this tale because they're unquestionably relevant to my life. But are sound and sentiment as significant as lineage? There are relatives by blood and relatives by affection. Sometimes the affection connections are more influential than the blood connections. In the end, we're all connected in some way even if we don't want to be, so we might as well claim whoever we want.

Ok, some of these people are still alive and maybe you think it misguiding to use a category like "dead" cavalierly. It's a category we'll all fall into sometime, and (I believe) many times. Think of it in purely scientific terms: gravity pulls us into the earth, holds us on the planet. Because we have mass, and we're spinning around in space, other objects in the universe are pulling us toward them. This makes us, mere humans, the connecting link between heaven and earth. Talk about being connected! In the end, you might say that the universe wins. Even if we come back, which I believe we do, we're pulled out again and again. So "dead" is a category for everybody. And "connections" are unavoidable.

~

**HOW DO WE KNOW SOMEONE HAS DIED?**
**SOMEONE ALWAYS DIES.**

~

A lot of people died in the sixties. Not only rock stars, but guys you went to high school with. What was a small town guy (or girl) to do? There weren't any jobs to be had and, for a lot of people, no other way to get training or an education if you don't want to end up on Relief. There was no way to get out of a town like Smiggle's other than join the Army (Navy, Marines). It's the only hope for some folks. So boys, and some girls, went from one end of the world, Smiggle's Bottom, to the other end of the world, Vietnam, and ended up with their name on a monument in Washington, D.C.

I didn't go to those funerals either. I didn't even know who got killed until I went to my Ten Year high school reunion.

~

Not all Smiggle's kids got blown away by guns. I had a friend in high school, Ruth Strange. Not only did she have an unfortunate last name, but she was overweight and had a tendency to grow facial hair. Her mother died when she was ten and her father, at a loss for advice to offer a pubescent daughter in crisis, convinced her to shave. Of course, this made her beard grow in thicker and resulted in five o'clock shadows and set Ruthy up for unmerciful ridicule in high school. Puberty is harsh but it was Hell for Ruthy.

During my freshman year in college, Ruthy got a job at a local lumber yard, lost sixty three pounds and figured out a way to deal with her facial hair. OK, she still wasn't a beauty, but she looked infinitely better. She bought herself a car and started taking college classes at night. Boys talked to her.

Myrna (another old friend) and I tried to convince her to come to the Cape with us and get a summer job. Ruthy was skeptical.

She agreed to leave the decision up to the Ouija Board. The three of us placed our fingers lightly on the planchette. "Will Ruthy regret it if she doesn't spend the summer in P-town with us?" we asked. "Definitely," it said.

So Ruthy bought her first bikini and drove up to Provincetown in the "Summer of Love." It was culture shock for a girl who'd never left Smiggle's Bottom and who had been a target of scorn all through school. After two weeks, she decided to try a quieter town in the southern part of the Cape. On her way home from work one night, an eighteen-wheeler went out of control and smashed her to smithereens.

I've never touched a Ouija Board since.

~

## The Dead Boyfriend

Don't think this is about you if you didn't have a fatal illness. Don't think this is about you if you can't play the harmonica. Don't think this is about you if your hands haven't been to secret places. Don't think this is about you if you don't know the playlist. Don't think this is about you if you're alive now.

It wasn't the car that I went for, though if it's still around, it's definitely a prize, especially since they don't make them anymore and you took such good care of it...

You were much more alive than other boys, despite your illness. Your smile was puppy-dog cute and your eyes lit up at the smallest moments, moments no one else noticed, moments only I noticed. Not much got past you except when intermittent waves of illness washed over you, grasped your body with agonizing strength, strangled you till you reeled, fought for breath, and had to be taken to the hospital. No amount of probing or poisoning seemed to help for long and with each episode you grew thinner, knobbier, weaker—except for those eyes and that smile.

Then one day you disappeared and I wondered what we'd meant to each other. I don't remember saying good-bye.

Years passed and that smile snuck up on me now and again, that big doofy, comforting grin.

I wasn't strong enough to watch you suffer and deteriorate. But that grin stayed with me, like a Cheshire boy. I didn't think of what might be...I hoped for a miracle.

I hope you were around long enough to hear Bruce Springsteen, Tim's son Jeff, Tom Petty. You would have loved Tom Petty; he reminds me of you in a lot of ways...

Some spells can't be broken, they loom up in a faraway place, in the guise of a cleaning lady from your hometown. Fond memories flood back. Reminiscences are acknowledged with, "you know he died."

How could it be when I still see that smile? How could it not be with such an illness?

I had known in some locked chamber of my heart.

I hadn't known about the pictures that you kept under the bed. I know those old photos; I kept them too.

I wept at the thought of old photos. What comfort did you find in my smile? I would have offered more—not a life but a hand, a word.

When did we say good-bye?

I imagine a stone in a country place or a shady churchyard. I imagine a mother crying, a stoic father, a brother who could never measure up...

When my old roommate's boyfriend died, she cried and talked to the stars. She drowned her grief in tears and cheap beer. I kept a smile and some old photos.

I'm thankful for the life and love that I've had and have now. I'm thankful for having known you. You might trip in the hole some people leave and be left behind. You might never say goodbye.

~

We got used to death in the sixties. We couldn't help it; it was all around us. It was in our neighborhoods, on TV. What we learned about Time was this: that you have to grab it while you can. We didn't think we'd live forever; we thought it would be all over by the time we hit thirty. Some of us are surprised. You have to make the most of your time, even if you have a longer life than you thought you would. You should try to do something good during your life, even if it's small.

Unfortunately, a lot of us forgot this lesson.

I suppose I should mention sex since people tend to connect sex and death. I don't know why this is so; sex has always seemed pretty lively to me. What can I say? I avoided it for a long time because I didn't want to get stuck in Smiggle's Bottom with a

Smiggle's Bottom boy. I did it once because I thought I was getting too old to be a virgin and it didn't turn out well; I could do it better by myself.

When I finally fell "in lust," it turned out better than I could have imagined—and I have a pretty extensive imagination. The details would spice these stories up but my children might want to read this some day and I don't want to offend them. Anyway, sex is a whole other book.

I can't say that there were high school boys or many college boys that I lusted after. I went out with some of them grudgingly; young boys can be smelly and awkward. "Dates" suck. Some of these guys became friends; some are lost forever. Most of my crushes were on older men. It's ironic that I ended up with someone younger than me.

~

They say that if you remember the sixties well, you probably weren't there. I don't remember anything well; that's the kind of mind I have. It's probably best that the sixties, and part of the seventies, are foggy. I was awkward and inept. It was an exciting time and a frightening time. My generation was taking over. We thought we could straighten things out. We had big dreams. You see how that went.

What I remember is: hitchhiking, late nights, West Virginia, smoking pot and Marlboros, protests, sit-ins, playing in a jug band, Jumpin' Jerry sundaes (named after Jerry West, only found at Chico's in Morgantown, which is no more).

I saw Bob Dylan and Joan Baez play at the Syria Mosque in Pittsburgh; I saw The Velvet Underground at WVU's Student Union (Quite a scene! I'll bet Lou Reed remembered that one too). I saw James Brown, Bo Diddley, Led Zeppelin, Tim

Buckley (at Max's Kansas City and other places). I saw Cream at the Café Au Go Go, and a hundred other bands at various free, and not quite free, concerts and fire-trap clubs.

I did not go to Woodstock. I turned down the chance to go because I didn't want to get involved with the boy who asked me. I was already in love with Louis, who was in Spain for the summer and lived to tell the tale. I don't regret it—I've seen the movie.

I saw men walk on the moon at the Snake Rock Tavern in West Virginia. We'd waited all day for it to happen and finally, in abject hunger, went out to pick up a pizza. The Snake Rock was jammed with drunken hillbillies. It was our luck that Neil Armstrong couldn't wait till we got back to Bump Street to step onto the moon's surface. He had to do it just at that moment in the midst of hooting, hollering, hugging drunks with stale beer and greasy pizza in their hands. It will never be "moonlight and Champagne" for me; the food I connect with the moon is pizza and 3.2% beer.

~

While old high school friends, cousins, and rock 'n roll stars were dying off, I was in college, not studying much and falling in love. There's nothing like death all around to bring people together that wouldn't otherwise have run into each other or paid attention to each other. I can't even say it was "love" at first, as much as "recognition."

Here's that other life thing again; believe what you want.

The story is that Louis saw me in the library, but we're not really sure what Louis was doing in the library; he was not an ardent student. He says he was taking out *The Willie Mays Story*. That could be true. I, on the other hand, spent a great deal of my life hiding among books, which is not to say I was studying.

A mutual friend offered to "fix us up" but when he came to ask me I said, "No way! I don't do blind dates."

A few days later I got a phone call: "Hi, I'm Louis a friend of Felix he's a weird guy isn't he well I was wondering if you're not doing anything Friday maybe we could get together or something what'd ya think?" All in one breath.

Perhaps there was something about the breath capacity that intrigued me. There was something about the sound of the voice…a timid New York accent? How did that happen? At the time, I lived in an apartment with three roommates. The roommates had friends and boyfriends and one of them was president of SDS, so we always had mobs of people staying with us. I figured if I didn't like him I could lose him in the crowd.

"OK," I said. "I live on the north campus."

On Friday, a new Fellini movie was playing at the student union. Or was it *Bonnie and Clyde* at a drive-in? Whatever it was, everyone went to see it and to make a night of it at Oggies afterward with pinball, beer, and pickled eggs.

I didn't want to be left alone with this Louis character so I called another friend and bribed her to come and hang out with us.

I opened the door to a freckled guy with a shock of kinky red hair and three shirts. "Why are you wearing three shirts?" I asked (not, "Come in," "Good to meet you.")

He looked down at himself as if he hadn't realized what he had on. "The bottom two are dirty."

I couldn't have been more impressed.

"This is Liz," I said as I let him in.

He zeroed in on my collection of records. Every dime I

could squeeze out went for records or books and they were loved and cared for. Louis was suitably reverent.

"I have this one too. I have this one. I can't believe you have this one! I've been looking for it everywhere." Music and multiple shirts were the talismans by which we recognized each other from other lives.

The recognition was immediate; love came later. I wished I hadn't invited Liz but it was like she wasn't there anyway. We talked all night. Liz made us food and drinks, emptied the ashtrays periodically. (Those were the days people smoked, a habit I was never overly committed to and ended long ago.)

The next weekend we went to Philadelphia and when we came back, he moved in.

We've been together ever since (as we have been in many lives before).

1. Did Bowie smoke?

# Chapter 7

## Fairy Tales, Legends, Golf: How My Parents Went...

Beware of fairy tales. The real ones are dark and brutal. For instance:

There once was a land called Xirðneh, the land of the gooð King Jmiji. Alas, King Jmiji was just a figurehead. He had no power at all. The real power lay with the evil minister, Roarso and his devious conspirator, Zog.

Jmiji had a son, Prince Snim, who fell in love with a peasant girl. The girl, Agia, was not aware of the political situation as she had been kept close to home all her life by loving parents who didn't trust King Jmiji to protect them from the evil afoot in the land.

When Agia discovered that Snim was a prince, she ran away to a town on the other side of the Mountains of Nagrom. (Running away was the customary method of dealing with complications in this culture.)

She made a meager living taking care of children until her best friend was struck by a sun flare and told Snim where she was, thinking he was a childhood friend willing to take Agia's dog to her.

Snim trudged through mountains and crossed raging rivers to find Agia. He took her back to the castle and King Jmiji loved her and taught her all his songs. In order to harass them, Roarso and Zog prepared a grand wedding for the couple and invited all the successful villains and lechers of the kingdom. The royal cooks prepared a grand banquet of dragon wings, firefly soup, prairiewolf in monkroot broth, anismold in figwort, iced bloodmint and many other delicacies.

Enim and Agia did not want such an elaborate affair, but they went along with it in order to appease Roarso and Zog, in the hope that they would soften their hold on the kingdom and allow good King Jmiji to see to the welfare of the people.

Enim and Agia were allowed a short honeymoon by the Citnalta Sea and when they returned they were put into separate dungeons. Although the dungeons were deep in the bowels of the castle, Agia could hear Enim shrieking and flailing from her cell. The situation was grim and went on for years. Jmiji died and Roarso took the country to war. Thousands were killed and the countryside fell into chaos.

In his dark cell, Enim was only given sweet things to eat and all his teeth fell out. His dark, shiny hair turned grey and sparse.

Agia was given only bitter herbs and seeds to eat, so she became weaker and weaker. There was one tiny shaft of light that penetrated her cell in the afternoons and she went blind from staring at it. When she died they fed her, piece by piece, to Enim.

~

THIS IS THE WAY REAL FAIRY TALES END. NO ONE EVER LIVES "HAPPILY EVER AFTER;" THAT'S A DISNEY INVENTION. YOU DO NOT WANT YOUR LIFE TO BE A FAIRY TALE. (AND THIS MAY BE WHY OTHER LIVES ARE OFFERED TO US.)

~~

When you marry, you accrue a great many more relatives

than you began with. This is unavoidable unless you marry an orphan and even they often come with adopted families. You'll like some of these people; the rest, you have to put up with just like you put up with your own irritating kinfolk. Think of your children; they'll have to learn to put up with both sides, the whole collection of lunatics. But don't worry, it's good for children to learn to deal with all kinds of people and the combat training-grounds for that are family holidays.

Funerals, on the other hand, are infinitely easier. People are less likely to argue or become abusive when they drink at funerals. (The key phrase here is "less likely;" it's not a certainty.) Most people are on their best behavior and memories that come up tend to be less grudging. (Though, occasionally, an old woman gets angry.)

~

The first funeral my own children attended was for Louis' favorite Uncle. I hadn't been to a funeral in a long time, but if my mother was right and funerals were for the sake of the bereaved, I thought I'd better make it to this one for Louis' sake.

 Uncle Mark was a "good 'ole boy" in a clan that bred serious worriers and tireless complainers. He was a happy mailman who knew everyone on his route and drank enough to be content with his lot in life but not enough to be a problem. He had a wife who loved to hear about the people he saw every day and two happy

teenaged daughters (I know, it doesn't happen often). When they weren't in high school, the daughters sang in a band called Albany, that covered sixties songs by groups like KC and the Sunshine Band, The Fifth Dimension—you get the picture. They both wanted to be veterinarians and saved every stray dog or cat they could round up (and a few birds).

Uncle Mark had never been sick in his whole life until he came down with mystifying flu-like symptoms one day in his fifties. He called it the Discount Flu because his doctor put him in a private room at the hospital and every prominent physician in the area came to see him and try to figure out what was going on inside him. Because he was a mystery they were interested in solving, they didn't charge him extra. He enjoyed the attention. After walking twenty miles a day for twenty-three years, he said he felt like he was being put up in a luxury hotel. All he had to do was ring his buzzer and he got whatever he wanted. Obviously, he didn't feel much like eating but was thankful for the chance to have a good long rest and watch some baseball on TV.

The man had never taken a vacation beyond a day at Two Flags Adventure Park—where monkeys, in the "drive-through" zoo, nearly destroyed his car.

Unfortunately, Uncle Mark did not lay up for very long. Within a week, all his organs failed and to this day no one knows why.

Louis took it very hard.

So did all the people on Uncle Mark's route, and in his neighborhood, and from his childhood, and everyone even remotely related to him. The funeral was a mob scene and you couldn't walk through the little house afterward. There was enough food to feed a small country and neighbors brought more each day of *shiva*. Childhood friends laughed over youthful antics and more recent friends recounted his bumbling kindness. Women in costume jewelry and uncomfortable shoes, men in short-sleeved shirts and cheap haircuts comforted each other with affection and cake. These are the signs of an admirable life.

Grief was relegated to obscure corners. It would be stumbled on in later years to confer sharp heart-piercing moments of regret now and again, over what might have been had he survived the mysterious illness and seen both his daughters become doctors, or teach his grandchildren the fine art of baseball.

~

This was near the time of John Lennon's death. John Lennon was the father of a child who was my own children's age. We lived on New York's Upper West Side, near them. We saw them in the park and on  the street. My daughter went to pre-school with Sean. To my children, John Lennon was less of a Beatle, more "Sean's dad."

This brought up a slew of questions.

"Will someone shoot our dad?" "Not very likely; your dad is not such a prominent figure." "Why did that guy want to kill Sean's dad?" A stumper.

And the all-time favorite: "What happens to you when you die?" "No one knows for sure, but here are the options…"

"Do you really believe we come back?" "I know dad and I have, and I'm pretty sure you've been here before."

~

Here's what I want played at my own funeral: "Knockin' on Heaven's Door"—the Dylan version. It's not that I don't like the Guns 'n Roses version, but it doesn't seem appropriate for a funeral unless you've been some kind of gangster, which I'm not. (Though I do like to think there's a little outlaw in me.) And "I Shall be Released" by The Band. Then something to cheer the people up, something they can all sing along to like "Sargent Pepper," or "Shout." I haven't decided.

~

My son ran into Sean Lennon a few weeks after the murder.

"How sad are you?" he asked Sean.

~~

Some deaths don't surprise you at all. This is true of Richard Manuel from The Band. Brian Jones. Keith Moon. Janis was very sad, but no surprise.

Other people surprise you by staying alive: Keith Richards, William Burroughs (that he stayed alive so long), Nancy Reagan (she must be 150 at this writing). How did Liz Taylor keep bouncing back?

~

At my own mother's funeral the talk was mostly of "golf."

Golf had always seemed a silly game to me. Actually, not having a competitive nature, most games seem pointless to me. People get that zealous look in their eye and I'm happy to say "Gee, if it's that important to you, you win." It would save a lot

? Cora ?

of sweat and sports injuries if everyone felt the same. Watching people compete seems even more pointless. How do you care enough to root for one person/team or another? It's a lot like voting; one lie is as good as the next—well, maybe not always.

I don't know much about golf, but having been a witness to its effect on my mother, I can tell you this: there is definitely something mystical about it. It's played in units of magic numbers: nine, eighteen. It involves all the basic elements of the universe, earth, metal, water, wood; the fire of sun cooks these ingredients or allows them to cool, and the result is a complex otherworldly magma. In its way, golf is a lot like yoga. It begins as a purely somatic exercise but its mystical design and esoteric mechanics conspire to produce a spiritual experience in people who are open to it. Like yoga, not everyone is open to the universal aspects and many people continue to practice in a shallow manner, stubbornly rejecting the spirit for what is known as "The 19th Hole," which negates the mystical numerology and numbs the soul. This is dangerous. Beware of these people. It seems to happen more often in golf than yoga as the alchemy of golf is much more subtle.

Before my mother took up golf, she was naïve to the ways of the world, protected from the harsher aspects of life. The occasional story of unwed pregnancy or adultery that filtered down to her (she was not a gossip), shocked and embarrassed her. She expected a certain amount of fraud from public officials and wealthy businessmen, but she had "nice" friends, upstanding women who kept their personal troubles to themselves. After all, this was not the big city. She wasn't unaware of the extent of misery that was called down upon unwary people, but she didn't think such things befell people she knew, as they were not spoken of among civil people.

The alchemical relationship of elements and magic numbers in golf (two letters away from "gold") encourage confession and sympathy in sensitive people. My mother played in golf leagues at public courses deep in the country. Occasionally, a group of them would travel to suburban realms to play. She met all kinds of women. She listened to their stories and helped them cope. She learned to be accepting of people who'd made mistakes and wrong choices. She learned to think for herself; she learned to think about herself. She gave up compulsive homemaking, left dishes in the sink, laundry unfolded, dinners unplanned. When I was a child, we used to have to dust and vacuum every day. We laughed when I reminded her of this later in life.

M's recurrent dreams were of flying. Perhaps she'd been a bird in another life and longed to return to the skies. At last she had taken off.

My father sat back in shock. He didn't dare complain, after fifty years of homemade meals, that they'd be eating at Drive 'n Dine four times a week. Actually, my father liked fast food. He'd had his fill of roast beef, mashed potatoes and gravy. He wanted hot dogs with mac and cheese.

So golf was the main topic at her funeral; the mystical aspects were not spoken of aloud, but that was the undertone. Nine holes doubled equals 18, the Hebrew letter chai, which means "life." How many nines are there in a human lifetime? How many lifetimes in a human?

We aim for emptiness in meditation. In order to achieve a meditative state, we are told to concentrate on something specific—our breath or the flame of a candle. What's the difference between aiming your mind or aiming a small, irregularly-surfaced ball for a designated hole/void, removing it, and setting your sights on the next void? Is it the eternal pursuit of Emptiness? Or a quest to fill the Void of the human condition? You begin to consider both.

The five elements create and destroy. When the combination is exact, the fire ignited, the numbers add up to the sum of a life, the iron heart can turn to gold. What happens to a heart that begins as gold? A golden heart filled with outside impurities in multiples of nine...

My mother was not playing against the other ladies; she was playing against time. Her time was called in the course of the game—but isn't everyone's?

What game are you playing?

~

My father mourned her for six years (another magic number). He hadn't been as ardent a golfer as my mother, but he couldn't bring himself to play the game at all after she died, so he marked time practicing magic tricks and shining his shoes until he was stroked.

~

Afterward, I held his rubbery hand in the hospital. Days went by, nights...a last tortured gasp after which he exhaled his sorrow and fell into peace.

Death is not accurately portrayed on TV. The blip on the

machine doesn't completely straight-line when the doctor calls an end to life. There are still a few faint blips at wide intervals. Believe me, I asked about this. "Just random electrical impulses..." he said. But a life is constructed of electrical impulses. I chose to wait with him till they stopped.

Immediately after death the spirit goes to a familiar place. In my father's case, this was his house. I returned to what I thought would be an empty house; I thought it would be eerie, depressing.

It was sunrise. Streams of bright sunlight illuminated every corner. Years of grief, which had dominated the house, were dissipated by the light of that morning. There was a sensation of release that made me feel guilty at first. Then I realized the feeling of release was not coming from me, but from him. It didn't lighten the heaviness of loss to know that I had lost him long before, when he lost her.

~

I was middle-aged when my father died, but I thought back to the third grade and Ruthann, who lost her father then. The third grade was not easy for any of us in Smiggle's Bottom. The Catholic kids who attended the Immaculate Conception School were just learning about the horrible tortures awaiting sinners, and memorizing catechism and jump rope chants.

Those of us in public school were stuck with Miss Haugh. In Miss Haugh's defense, those days the only occupations open to women were teaching, nursing, and secretarial work. Miss Haugh, not being nurse or secretary material and unable to find a husband to support her, was stuck in the field of teaching. She was not happy.

She was a grim woman with thick ankles who wore shapeless, colorless clothing. She didn't like children—with the exception of Malinda Wiltrout. Malinda Wiltrout cleaned the erasers, complimented Miss Haugh on her hair and blouses, and "told" on everyone. Malinda Wiltrout and I came to blows on the playground over a minor point in a Sky King episode and that finished me with Miss Haugh. Miss Haugh didn't see fit to break up the fight right away and Malinda, who outweighed me by twenty pounds, punched me in the stomach so hard that I threw up on Willard Henry's shoes—possibly the only ones he had.

It didn't help that I'd gone into the girls' bathroom the day before singing, "Ole Miss Haugh is a bag of tough stuff and she huffs and puffs all day." Miss Haugh burst out of her stall just as I hit the chorus.

My report card went from "Es" (excellent) to "Ss" (satisfactory) and "Us" (unsatisfactory). We nearly drowned in homework and she took my report on itchy sweaters, crunched it up into a ball, and threw it at me.

Most kids were reduced to tears routinely and Melva Brothers actually peed her pants in reading group when Miss Haugh wouldn't give her a bathroom pass. Everyone felt bad for Melva and no one made fun of her except Malinda Wiltrout. We were all hoping Miss Haugh would have to clean it up, but she called Mr. Kunkle, the janitor, to do that.

~

The summer after third grade there was an invasion of beetles. Kids took vengeance for the anguish of the school year by torturing and killing these insects. Adults encouraged this rampage as the beetles threatened trees and shrubbery.

~

Fourth grade was infinitely better. Miss Vodge was a gift. The fourth and fifth grades were combined because of a shortage of rooms and teachers, and we got to reenact the Civil War in the hallway against fifth graders. Miss Vodge told us gruesome stories about how the wounded soldiers were mutilated by doctors without anesthesia. It was great fuel for imagination and cursing people we didn't like.

Malinda Wiltrout could not seduce Miss Vodge with her compliments and was relegated to the last reading group next to Henry Little who smelled awful and fell asleep all the time. They cut all her hair off because she got headaches from the weight of it, and that finally shut her up for good.

I was in the first reading group, but I had a terrible secret. I couldn't tell time.

No one in our town had heard of digital clocks, and numbers, especially arranged in a circle in odd units—five, twelve, sixty— unnerved and confused me. I couldn't make any sense of it. Big hands, little hands, I could never remember which was which and I didn't understand the point of time anyway. If it was dark and you were tired, it was bedtime. If you were hungry, eat; why wait? Your mother made sure you were at school on time and the teachers told you when to go home.

My inner world was timeless and that was where I spent most of my time. This was one of the more embarrassing consequences: Miss Vodge would send me out into the hall to consult the big clock for her. I'd look for Mr. Kunkle or wait on the stairs, out of sight, until an older kid or teacher walked by and ask them for the time. That I was gone longer than it took to walk to the end of the hall and look up at the clock was not an issue, as I was often lost in fantasy and Miss Vodge was tolerant of a certain amount of daydreaming.

~

Often, I was not daydreaming at all, but in a perfect meditative trance, mind clear, thinking of nothing. Grown-ups and other kids inevitably interrupted with, "a penny for your thoughts." Or, "What are you thinking about?" If I told them the truth, "nothing," they scoffed. "Only idiots have brains that stop working." I didn't want them to know I was an idiot so I made up stuff, "Dracula," "giraffes," "supper."

Now I'm told that it's a state to be strived for but I can't seem to sustain it at this age. My dog, Puppet, was an excellent mediator.

~~

Through all of this, good and bad, Pop was my best friend. He helped me with Miss Haugh's homework. He listened to the Civil War stories I brought home. He ultimately taught me how to tell time and a lot of other stuff. He was my buddy until I reached puberty, then he stopped telling me stories and wouldn't hold my hand; I didn't dare try to climb into his lap. He seemed to think that everything I did was either stupid or irritating. I was as confused by him as he was by me. M tried to intervene, but neither of us wanted to hear what she had to say. She ultimately gave up and drifted into her own menopausal fugue for a few years. We grew apart.

After M was gone, he was always sad. We ate fast food together because he didn't like my cooking, didn't understand rice or bread that wasn't white, or vegetables that crunched. We didn't ask each other what we were thinking.

# Chapter 8

## Carnivals

When I was young, the carnival was allowed to come to our town once a year. Carnivals are mystical things, but in a different way than golf. Carnivals, in those days, existed on the edge of Evil. That's not to say that carnies are evil people themselves, not any more so than bookkeepers or beauticians or plumbers. But they have a way of bringing out evil in (alleged) "normal" people. This happens because the sounds, smells, and images invoked by a carnival atmosphere unleash synaptic responses that affect neurons, membranes and fluids of the brain, triggering atypical hormones that release impulses from deep within the subconscious, dark places people avoid admitting they have, and never go to.

This is why it's important to acknowledge your dark places; crawl into them and look around; open the blinds and let the sunlight in. I'm not advocating murder or abject perversion here. I'm just saying, go out and play a violent video game, see a horror movie, read some porn or some old fairy tales, get it out of your system. Children, especially, need vicarious violence in their lives. Think about it, they're powerless; frustration and resentment builds up, especially in the teen years and they're prohibited from doing anything about it. It's not video games and loud music that cause them to detonate; it's what parents, teachers, clergy, the world does to them and the frustration of being helpless to stop it or even tell anyone about it. It's about not being listened to or respected or understood. It's about being ignored except when you do something "wrong."

Violent video games are nothing new. Kids have always loved violence. Think about the old fairy tales: little girls who put on shoes and are forced to dance in them forever, children who push an old woman into a fire rather than be eaten by her. When I was a kid we had *Tom and Jerry*, *The Road Runner*, *Sylvester and Tweety*, *Bugs Bunny*, cartoon characters that routinely blew each other up or dropped pianos on each other's heads.

It's a complicated subject that I feel strongly about but we won't go there now.

~

Let's go to an old-time carnival instead, listen to the tacky music, smell the food frying—nothing smells better than food fried in well-used fat. Eat enough spun sugar to make you sick to your stomach, and look around.

I was never much for carnival rides. The food made me nauseous and I wasn't good at going around in circles. One or two rides were enough to put me away. And I knew better than to play the games. My dad was a magician and an ex-huckster (with a very straight day job); he knew how such things were rigged to the disadvantage of "marks."

"Hey, Red," they'd call out to him. "Come over here and win the kid a kewpie."

"No thanks, I used to run one of these games."

They'd give him a little salute or a wink and stop bothering him.

I was allowed to go into the fun house, but never the Freak Show. I became obsessed with what might go on there.

Mr. Ondik at the bank had rickets when he was a child. It left him dwarfed and crippled. His crutches pushed his

shoulders up so high that he had no neck and his hearing was affected. Mrs. Junic, our biology teacher, had a hump on her back. Porky Bigham only had one eye and a lid that closed over an empty hole. Mrs. Halfhill's brother was hunchbacked and a dwarf and he had a wife and three kids. Sharon Nickelson had a withered arm; James Alona had a club foot. Annie Oakley was "retarded" (we were allowed to use that term in those days) and walked around with toy guns—there was a whole room of "retarded" kids in our school in various stages of drool and deformity. They were pretty much taken for granted, teased by the same kids that bullied everyone else. None of these people were considered "challenged." Many of them were upstanding members of our community; they delivered papers, bagged groceries, and swept out stores. (Pumping gas was a middle-class occupation—just to give you the whole picture.)

The spectrum of accepted humanity was vast, so what kind of creatures could possibly constitute a Freak Show, I wondered. I was aware of a lot of variations, but considered none of them "freaks." What horrible abominations were there roaming the outside world? I wanted to see seal boys and alligator men, people who ate live chickens and rodents. I'd seen women who were enormously fat and had beards. I wanted to see creatures who were part animal or vegetable or mineral. I wanted to see turtles with two heads, goats with six legs. Then again, I didn't want to see them.

It didn't really matter; I wasn't allowed.

Years later, my aunt Katharine got cancer and turned to stone. I didn't see this myself because she lived in Texas by then, but M went down to help care for her and she said that only Aunt Kat's eyes moved and that her skin was hard and dry. Aunt Kat had always been sedentary anyway—you even ate meals on little metal trays in front of the TV when you visited her—so becoming a rock was not a great leap.

For a while, though, she was the closest thing to a real freak our family had to offer.

~

I often thought of running off with a carnival. It has to be great traveling the country with people whose deformities were on the outside. I've known plenty of folks who were deformed on the inside; I think this is much more serious.

Louis' Aunt Linnea and her friends have had dozens of "cosmetic" surgeries. Most of them look less human than the seal boy or the puppet woman but they're not considered freaks. Go figure.

Some people want to be known as freaks. Some people gave "freaks" a bad name. There's an enormous number of elaborate variations on the human theme. None of these are easy to live with. One person's freak is another person's normal.

~

I've wonder what Louis and I would do if we were to join a carnival. Louis is not good at fixing things, so we couldn't run a ride. But he'd make a good manager. I could mend costumes and tents, and see that everyone was fed some decent food. I used to help Pop in his magic act but I'm not young enough to be a magician's assistant now. Still, if our acts were exotic enough, Ricky Jay would come to see us and write about our show.

Ricky Jay is a magician, specifically a card manipulator. He's the little strange guy in David Mamet movies and early "Deadwood" episodes. He's very brilliant in a weird sort of way. He writes books about freaks and conmen and his rotting dice collection. If I was to win a contest and the prize was that I could have dinner with any famous person in the world, it would be Ricky Jay—not Johnny Depp though it would be tempting, and certainly not Bob Dylan; that would be way too intimidating. (But if they want to have dinner with me, I wouldn't say no.)

~

HERE'S SOMETHING ONLY LOUIS KNOWS ABOUT ME: MY DREAMS HAVE THEME SONGS.

~

My cousin Leanor was a carnival in a cake pan. She was over six feet tall. She played guitar, piano and spoons without ever taking a lesson. She had a way of stuffing an upright piano with newspaper to make it sound honky-tonk. She could really belt out a tune.

Three days before her wedding, she plopped her diaphragm down on the dining room table for all us younger kids to see. And she necked with her fiancé all through Thanksgiving dinner because, "It's OK now, we're engaged."

Leanor's job was making cakes. She made cakes in the shape of antique cars, wildcats, hand grenades (I swear) and all kinds of other stuff. I have a picture of me when I was seven, holding a lamb-shaped cake she made for my birthday. Some of her cakes were five feet tall and had to be carried in pieces and assembled at weddings. They tasted good too—which doesn't always happen.

Her only fault was that she was closed-minded, right-wing and a bigot. There was no use trying to talk her out of it. I tried a few times and gave up. It was better to limit the conversation to cake and honky tonk.

Leanor was not quite sixty when she died. She took shark cartilage to get rid of her cancer but all it did was turn her hair greenish. She liked the green so much that she started talking about getting tattoos on her legs to hide her varicose veins. She never got well enough to do this.

The funeral was pretty boring: country church, sedate hymns, no hysterics, no good stories. I went with my very favorite cousin Cora. Cora was Leanor's twin sister, but she was very different—short and studious, liberal and open-minded. She favored mints over cake, always had some with her, and smelled great because she chewed on them constantly. She was a little fat and not musical at all.

Cora had four boys that went into the army. One got killed in Indonesia, where there was no war that anyone knew of. One came back crazy and when her husband died, she was stuck with him since she had no money to send him away and couldn't bear to put him in a "government home." The other two went to college on the army and became teachers.

Cora put herself through school and became a kindergarten teacher. She said that all kids were wonderful up until the age of five, but after kindergarten they became brats, and life was too short to spend dealing with grown-ups or brats. She wasn't popular with parents because she told them exactly what she thought and cut them off when they asked her about why she taught units on "icky things" and read them violent stories. The kids, however, loved her—and "icky things"—and violent stories. The parents were mostly too busy to do more than complain.

Cora did not suffer fools, but for some reason she liked me and I'm about as big a fool as there is. I was ten years younger than her and she liked me as a child and as a teenager who babysat her children and helped her around the house—which was always a mess. All the relatives complained about her messy house but she didn't give a damn. Four young boys can wreak quite a bit of havoc and you're better off seeing that they don't kill each other, than washing the dirty dishes. That was Cora's attitude. "If it bothers you so much, just don't come here," she told people. She was happy to take her boys for a free meal at anyone else's house.

Cora got cancer too; three years after Leanor. They gave her one year with treatment, six months without. She decided against the year of torture and went without treatment. She gave away all her stuff, found a place for the crazy son, and lived with another son and his family in Goodish, West Virginia until the end. She lasted a year anyway.

I didn't see her that last year, I was busy with my own small children in New York. But I talked to her on the phone a few times. She kept herself busy playing with her granddaughters and writing to world leaders telling them how they'd fucked things up. She took a lot of drugs and told me how much she liked them and regretted she hadn't taken them in the sixties. "Perhaps it was because you had young children at the time," I said. "I could have handled it," she said.

I'm glad she was able to enjoy herself; she deserved it after the difficult life she'd led. Luckily, her son lived in West Virginia instead of southwestern Pennsylvania. Mines and mills had destroyed the magic in Pennsylvania hills, but West Virginia hills were alive and well at that time and had plenty of magic. It was a decent place to live and a pretty good place to die. I'm not sure about now, after they've fracked places to death and blown the tops off mountains.

People there know how to put on a funeral. They have good singers and good pickers. Cora had the time to plan the details of a funeral. She mulled over the options of music, speeches, a cozy plot under a shade tree. She decided against everything except the plot under a tree. She didn't want a funeral at all but there's nothing like a crazy son to liven up an un-funeral. He danced and sang and spoke in tongues. He scared all the old church ladies at the cemetery that were decorating the graves for Hootie Holt's birthday (I don't know who he is either). These were ladies that Cora wouldn't have wanted to be around anyway. Her stone has her name and dates and one sentence, "Don't throw blocks."

~

I want my stone to say, "Watch out!"

~

Or maybe, "She told good stories."

~

Or, "Here we go again."
I can't decide.

~

Going to funerals makes you see things differently; makes you step back and take in the big picture. Like sitting on the moon, everyone and all their troubles look small and far away, even your own. Time stretches out around you. You can see the line of a life, your own and others. It's not like ironing when you do one thing and

think of all kinds of other things. And its not like dropping the Thanksgiving turkey on the floor and you have to think quick about what you're going to do to get it on the table without anybody knowing.

Some people get philosophical when they face death. Cora didn't. She just lived, one moment at a time. Will I be able to keep breakfast down? Do I have enough energy to play Chutes and Ladders with my granddaughter? Those kinds of things.

I thought Cora would have been the one to go down kicking and screaming. Go figure.

~

When Cora's sister, Leanor, died, all the relatives stayed in the same Super 8 motel and spent the night before the funeral drinking and watching line dancing on cable TV. Cora and I looked in for a few minutes and then went back to our room and talked until 4:00 a.m.

No one would have dared watch line dancing at Cora's funeral, if she'd had one. Cora wasn't a dancer and she was the sort of person that would come back and haunt you if you did something she didn't like. She didn't ask for much other than a little respect. What she got, she worked hard for.

But some people deserve better than they get.

~

Mostly, I try not to question death. Not even when I think it's come unfairly. What good does it do?

# Chapter 9

## Dogs

Lucy was my one true dog companion. Other dogs in my life either had to be taken away because they caused asthma attacks or they attached themselves to my children. When we got our first dog, my asthma came back as an adult. My children would rather have gotten rid of me than the dog, so I gave myself allergy shots every week for thirteen years. When my husband closed his business, we had to change our health insurance and the new one wouldn't pay for antigens. My allergies never came back. The shots laid the foundation, and practicing tai chi ch'uan had strengthened my immune system.

I didn't tell Lucy about my previous dogs, but I can tell you. (Cat people can skip over this part.)

Boots was a mutt puppy my dad brought home when I was five. I stopped breathing when he came into the house and Pop rushed me to the hospital and took Boots back to the shelter he came from. I don't want to think anything bad happened to that puppy; he was pretty cute so I'm sure someone adopted him and gave him a good home. I hope he had a happy life. He probably wouldn't have been safe in the Fourgoose house anyway with Freddy Fourgoose around. Freddy was capable of sadistic behavior and I couldn't have watched Boots every second of every day.

Bowser was a Golden Retriever we adopted when our kids were young. Our kids named all of their pets Bowser even though the ones before had been mostly fish—and a bird. We hadn't had much luck with pets before the canine version of Bowser entered our lives. The fish always died and funerals over the toilet get old quickly.

Bowser the bird, flew out the window one evening just before supper. We don't know how the cage door got open, but Bowser was no Houdini. I had to take two screaming toddlers in their pajamas out into the streets of New York City to look for him while the vegetables turned brown and soggy on the stove. There were a lot of sympathetic commuters, but no sign of a parakeet. The vigil went on for weeks, every time we went outside.

There are birds of prey living in Manhattan. I didn't tell my children.

We didn't have any pets for a long time after that.

Then Bowser the dog came along; he was the dumbest dog that ever lived. It took years to get him housebroken and he never learned one trick although we all worked at teaching him, but who cares? He was game for anything two little thugs could think up. My son used him as a pillow or a footrest. My daughter dressed him up in ridiculous costumes and built obstacle courses for him to run through. He loved every moment of it.

When he got tired, he went to the only place he could find quiet, an old armoire with a broken door. The kids would get him so exhausted that only a faint thumping of his tail greeted you as you walked by.

After he died, we often heard thumping coming from that armoire.

One night Louis was walking him in the park when a black car whizzed by and hit the dog. (We're lucky he missed Louis.) Bowser flew ten feet up in the air and came down with an ominous thud. The car kept going. My traumatized husband managed to get a doorman to call me to come with the car. We got him to the vet, followed by police who couldn't figure out what a car was doing in the park after closing time.

Bowser didn't make it and my son, who was in college at the time, wanted to quit school and come home to raise puppies. (It took all of us and his girlfriend to talk him out of it.)

We had Bowser cremated, but no one could decide what to do with the ashes. They sat on a shelf through two moves. When both kids were out of college and moving into their own places, Louis and I decided it was time for us to move again. I put my foot down about Bowser's ashes. The four of us took the ashes out to the country for a proper release.

This is the measure of the hold the dead have on the living and the power they compel in the universe: When we finally found a suitable place, we all got out of the car. There was a crack of thunder and the heavens let loose. None of us could speak. We stood in the rain, with a tin of dog ashes that had been sitting around for five years, and bawled. Finally, I opened the bag and ashes blew all over us, turning to mud in the rain.

~

## Lucy

I hate it when creatures up and die on you, especially when that creature was your best friend and seemed fine one day and just stopped eating the next and when you took her to the vet, he just shook his head and came out with BAD news and no hope. I hate it when

they get scary sick really fast, like in a week they can't move, have trouble breathing, shit black bile and throw up blood by the pint. I hate it when you try to sneak into another room to cry and they hike themselves up to follow and see what's wrong because that's their job — taking care of you, watching over you, laying on the floor at your feet, getting dog hair on your black pants. I hate it when you finally hold them in your arms and pay the vet to kill them. I don't believe in killing, but I couldn't watch that kind of suffering any longer. I was never responsible for the death of any creature bigger than a fly before that.

I hate coming home to a quiet house, no tail wagging, no wet kisses, but some creatures cannot be replaced. Crumbs stay on the floor until ants intercede and I have to kill more creatures. Sometimes I hear breathing under the bed where she used to sleep...but there's only a small tin of ashes.

# Chapter 10

## Water, Widows, and Rehab

Water was a large part of my life even though I never saw the ocean until I was nineteen years old. When I saw it, I was overwhelmed. I don't know how anyone lives by the ocean. It's a sentient mountain of uncontrollable and powerful energy lashing out at you, crashing toward you, eating away at the land you stand on, spitting out sand and salt to corrode and erode everything in the neighborhood, spitting out driftwood and shells and refuse.

My mother's ancestors were river people. My Manx grandmother crossed a great ocean to settle on the banks of an obscure river. I was carved out of my mother in a place where three rivers converged. When we were well enough to travel, my father took us to the banks of the Youghiogheny. As a child I played on the riverside, swirling the oily colors in the water with a stick. I swam in it; washed my hair in the rapids, watched it dry up and swell.

Rich people lived on high ground where floods couldn't reach; the rest of us took our chances on the banks. Whole towns were swallowed and given back, swallowed and given back. In bad storms, barges, loosened from their moorings, swept down the river and careened into bridges, destroying them. The bridges were rebuilt and we crossed and re-crossed the river. Crossing becomes second-nature. Valleys are carved out.

I can chant the names of rivers and lakes that chaperoned my life: Ohio, Allegheny, Monongahala, Monanghelia, Mississippi. Erie and Cheat and Chesapeake. Amazon, Mekong, Nile, Hudson, East, and now Harlem…. Each one a character of its own, a lesson in continuity, a unique adventure.

## Soundings

The river is restless. It scabbers at the rocks below, wills itself to vapor and rains down on me. I watch from the bank but see only turmoil and backwash. It'll be in a snit all night, swirling and gushing, eroding its banks to spite itself.

Memories trickle down my scalp with the drizzle and I hear Mrs. Hungerford in chemistry class telling us, "Water is an international solvent; in time it will wear away anything." In the back of the room, I giggle at Albert Star's imitation of Mohammad Ali's poetry (though he was Cassius Clay then). I'm more interested in butterfly and bee than chemistry. This is not my river. It's not the one I swam in as a child, jumped into from railroad bridges. It's not the one I threw cans in for target practice. My river carved a valley of childhood so deep that you couldn't see over the mountains it formed; we had to conjure a world from dreams. My grandfather died burrowing into the mountains for black coom, and all the water in all the rivers couldn't wash him clean. My river sparkled with rainbow resins and viscose hopes. It wore old Mrs. Hungerford down completely and delivered Albert Star. Some others drowned. I thought I'd never get away but dog-girls, like me, are persistent paddlers.

I know what it is to be liquid. I know what it is to puddle up and rest in low dark places. The river and I have much in common; it knows the illusion of me just as I know the changing reality of it. Not long ago, this river was so stunned by the coldness of the world that it nearly froze solid. It grew stiff and hard, the closest it will get to death. Villagers took pictures and published them in newspapers. My own river would never have done that, but it was known to swell and hurl boats and houses at bridges, knocking some of them down.

I strive to be water knowing full well that I will end up as dust. Bits of me are flaking off already. I've been called fire and I've been called air, but we always aspire to what we are not and I work hard at liquid, concentrating on waves and spirals, falling into whirlpools and emerging to pursue the flow.

The river may not pursue clarity or wish to have its depths explored; it may resent undue attention. It must loathe the contamination we've inflicted. Perhaps it's displeased that I'm such an inept disciple, for I'll never achieve the capacity to benefit all living things as water does.

Tomorrow it will settle back and become complacent, stretch out in the sun and give rides to birds.

~

I came close to drowning once, but it wasn't in a river. I was a child and went head-first into a crowded swimming pool. The water held me upside-down. I didn't panic. Perhaps I was too young to panic; too close to the memory of floating in the water of my mother. I opened my eyes and watched the other people around me moving slowly; they were liquid in liquid. It was like a dream. I don't know how long I was under the water. Someone finally thought to pull me up by my

feet. I choked a bit but my mother urged me to go right back into the pool.

I dream that I can breathe in water. Perhaps it's a memory of that day when I stayed alive under it. In my dream, I suck the air out of the tiniest bubbles; I move slowly, gracefully. Perhaps it's a memory of another life, a life before we crawled onto the land. My mother dreamt of flying; I swim through my dreams.

~

When summer air wafts through my window, I think of stars that I've seen in various skies, and holding hands, the quiet of it. I think of the ache aroused by the sound of distant train whistles, hands swollen with poison ivy, lightning bugs in Bell jars with holes punched in the lid. I hear secrets that were whispered to weeping willows, jump-rope chants, the tinkling melody of Ice Cream Ike's truck.

If you get into a swimming pool at night, the kind that has light shining up through the water, and there's darkness all around and you try to walk, then you can sense what it feels like to be stuck but not caught, straining to get somewhere while knowing you can always lay back and float. If you're sporting, you remember to splash.

~~

The old widow ladies in our town wore black. They were Italian and Slavic and once their husbands (or siblings, or parents) died they wore nothing but black clothing for the rest of their lives. Some of them wore thick black stockings even in the heat of summer. I knew some husbands of these women; they were the fathers of friends or had been owners of businesses in town. A few of them were brutal men and their death should have been occasions for rejoicing. This may sound like a cruel thing to say, but some walls are thin and in the summer, windows were kept open. There was no air conditioning—only in the movie theater, and that closed early on.

Faith Zavatsky lived above me in the Linden Hill Garden apartments. (This was not a hill where rich people lived even though it was well above the river.) We moved there from the Fourgoose house when I was eight years old. Mr. Zavatsky drank and beat on Faith routinely. He never touched her little sister who was angelic looking but nasty like her parents. While Mr. and Mrs Zavatsky sat outside on lawn chairs and drank beer, Faith cleaned the apartment, cooked, and did the all the dishes. She wasn't popular with the other kids because she was nervous, jittery, awkward. I was the only one who knew why.

One day I came home and Faith was sitting on my mother's lap crying. I wasn't jealous. I knew what she was up against and I'd always wanted a sister—even a nervous crybaby one.

She didn't come to live with us though. We moved to another apartment across the way. Faith Zavatsky's life would have been easier if her father had died. But he didn't.

~

The Italian ladies-in-black did a lot of cooking. They didn't bake bread and pies like my grandmothers, they made whole meals—great pans of pasta, that we called spaghetti back then, and meatballs. They gave this food away, to relatives and neighbors; they gave a lot of it to their churches. They were among the first to come to your door when someone died. It was as if they had ESP; they were at the door before funeral arrangements were made.

Another woman with this kind of ESP was Mrs. Coughenour. Mrs. Coughenour had a live husband but she preferred to spend her time with the bereaved. She could smell death from across town.

You couldn't say anything bad about her; she was sympathetic and helpful. But you didn't want to see her hovering around your neighborhood.

Mrs. Coughenour was big on casseroles and she wasn't the best cook around. She probably didn't have time to do more than throw a few things in a pan, slap some cheese and breadcrumbs over it, and dash out. She went home from neighbor's houses with other people's unfinished food for her husband, and was forever returning dishes all over town. She also took flowers home. She rearranged them and offered them to other bereaved families or kept them for herself. Occasionally, Mr. Coughenour, who seemed to have an eternal cold, would turn up at someone's house looking for his wife, and join the grieving family for a meal. But not very often. We didn't see much of Mr. Coughenour.

Mrs. Coughenour didn't go to funerals unless it was a very close relative; she sat in the bereaved family's home so they wouldn't get robbed while they were at the funeral. To my knowledge, there'd never been a robbery during a funeral in our town, but Mrs. Coughenour convinced everyone that thieves made their living reading the obituaries.

Mrs. Coughenour died before her husband, which must have pissed her off because if anyone knew how to throw a funeral, Mrs. Coughenour surely did and she would have thrown a doozy for her own husband if he'd had the decency to die first. Mr. Coughenour buried his wife the day after she died and put it in the paper afterward, presumably to keep the crowds away from his door. Neighbors that brought food and condolences after they saw the announcement were not invited inside.

Mr. Coughenour never allowed another flower to enter his house and his sniffles and sneezes disappeared. He dressed in pastel golf clothes and partook of the buffet at the Drive 'n Dine every night till the day he died.

~

Not everyone inspires condolences from their friends and neighbors.

Cousin Larry was murdered. Actually, Larry wasn't a first cousin to me; he was the second cousin of my blood-cousin—whatever that means. He was several years older and I only ever met him once, but he was talked about a lot.

Larry "ran with a bad crowd" and "sent his mother to an early grave." My aunt Pauline, who was his...oh, who knows what... only said these kind of general things and not much else. But the cousins and their friends who knew him from school, talked about him in more detail.

When he was eight he flushed his Fort Apache play set down the toilet and flooded the house. When he was ten he drove his father's Studebaker from Saltlick to Eighty Acres Road. He stole money out of ladies' purses, penny candy from stores; skate keys, 45 rpm records, pens and pencils from other kids. He dropped water balloons on the Fuller Brush man and the Avon lady, sniffed mimeograph paper at school, and ran away six times before he was fourteen.

When he was seventeen, his dad signed him into the Navy and it looked like he was "turning into a new leaf," as Aunt Pauline said. (This is a confusing thing to say to a child. Was he attached to a tree?) Then, when he was on leave in Pittsburgh, somebody shot him in the head and left him in an alley. The grown-ups wouldn't talk about it, but it didn't sound like they tried to find the murderer very hard. It wasn't even in our local paper and news about servicemen was a big deal in Smiggle's Bottom.

It was so hushed up that my mother and Aunt Pauline were the only relatives that went to his house after the funeral. The rest of the relatives didn't go to the funeral because they didn't want to "embarrass" his mother—who was in poor health and didn't last much longer after that.

I think it must have been a drug deal. His murder must not have been a "mystery" or the police would have come around and questioned us all. It was many years ago and a good time to be a drug dealer. All the whisperings about Larry reeked of drugs. If he would have lived today, they would have sent him to rehab instead of the Navy.

~

Sometimes I wish I did drugs so I could go to rehab. You get to take off for a month or more, eat healthy food, do crafts, and hang out with people who have interesting stories to tell. I think that if you're a good girl (or boy) for thirty or fifty years, the government should send you to rehab as a reward. Why should these vacations only be offered to drunks and druggies and gamblers? I'd be willing to make a few positive changes if I had time off and someone to show me how. I'd even be willing to clean the toilet or mop or whatever "horrible punishments" they make you do. (I do those things in my own house anyway.) I could sit around and drink coffee (they always drink coffee) and listen to people's stories and tell mine and meet famous people. Sounds pretty good to me.

~

OK, maybe I'm not such a good girl. I sniffed some mimeograph paper in my time. Hasn't everyone stolen something sometime in their life? Maybe not my dad, but pretty much everyone else. I never stole anything from a person or a small business, just very small things from very big companies. Insignificant stuff, really. I know you've stolen pencils and staples from your office and, is everything on your tax form true? (Of course it is, mine too.) And didn't you cheat on an algebra test once?

What goes on in your head when someone crosses you?

I try hard to be open to everyone, but there are people that get on my nerves. For a while I was bend-over-backward-nice to these people, but it never made them behave any better and I hate being a phony so I gave it up. Every once in a while when

I get really irritated, I tell them what assholes they are. And I don't feel one bit bad about it.

Once I threw all of Mrs. Crosby's clean towels off the line and stomped them into the dirt because she told M she saw me kiss Ray Dodrill in the garage.

I played with fire. (I still do this sometimes.)

My insurrections are usually pretty minor but I almost never get caught. So watch out.

## The Goddess That Wasn't

Venus and I were good friends in the sixth grade. We made bracelets out of old magazines and sold them to the other kids for pennies. We used the money to buy candy, which Venus mostly ate. Sixth grade was a pleasure because Miss Thompson was our teacher.

Venus lived near the school and I lived several miles away so I didn't see much of her in the summer. Everyone hoped Miss Malabader, the science teacher, would quit or be abducted by aliens because she was as mean as Miss Thompson was nice. But that didn't happen.

Venus wormed her way into Miss Malabader's black heart, but I didn't.

One day Venus invited me to lunch at her house. My mother had given me two nickels to buy popsicles from the man who sold them outside of school. I wasn't in the mood for a popsicle so, over peanut butter sandwiches in Venus' kitchen, I proposed that we use our money to buy a comic book. Venus refused and took great offense that I wouldn't have a popsicle with her. I gave her one nickel and told her I'd rather save my nickel until I accumulated enough for a comic. She had a fit—a screaming, throwing things, red in the face, out of control, tantrum. There were no adults around to mitigate the violence and it unnerved me so much that I ran out of the house, all the way home.

I was so upset that she'd carry on so passionately because I didn't want to do what she wanted me to do, and so exhausted by heat and exertion when I got home, that I threw up and my mother wouldn't let me go back to school that day.

When my other friends brought my homework that afternoon, they reported that Venus had come to school and told the class how I'd gone through her mother's dresser looking for money, broke things in her house, and kicked her blind grandmother. Miss Malabader said she wasn't surprised but my friends didn't believe I'd do anything like that. Apparently, they'd all had their doubts about Venus' integrity before this incident. My friend, Janis, called Venus a liar so Miss Malabader sent her to the principal, who let her read in the library for an hour in lieu of "punishment." I guess grown-ups had Miss Malabader's (and, I see now, Venus') number.

I stayed away from Venus for the rest of the year and when spring came a delivery man arrived with a bouquet of lilies for Miss Malabader. The card said, "with love from Felicity and Janis." Janis and I assured Miss Malabader and the rest of the class that we hadn't sent it. Miss Malabader stomped off in a huff to put her mysterious flowers in water.

"Venus the Rat," my friends and I whispered to each other.

We told our mothers and when the florist called my mother for the money, she refused to pay and told him to track down the person who ordered the flowers because it certainly wasn't her daughter. My mother was a mild woman but she wasn't a push-over. She knew when I was in the wrong and when it was time to stand up for me. And she knew that I would NEVER have sent flowers to Miss Malabader, nor anyone without asking her first. Janis' mother felt the same.

I went all through school with Venus and never spoke to her again. She was the only person for whom I held a grudge—though I wouldn't call it a grudge when I rarely thought about her.

Recently, I got an email from Janis asking if I knew that Venus died. I hadn't thought about her in years. I didn't know where she lived, what her life had been like and I didn't care. There was no grudge, no...anything.

So why do I feel bad?

# Chapter 11

## Finery, Funnery and the Fantastic

The meanest thing my mother ever did was this: A neighbor gave me a pair of her old red plaid Bermuda shorts when I was twelve. I loved those shorts and wore them all that summer and the next. By August of my fifteenth summer they were frayed and totally faded but they still fit as I had grown only a little taller, and no wider. M hated them. "You look like a ragamuffin," she told me. I'd never seen a ragamuffin but if they wore cool broken-in plaid shorts, I was all for looking like them.

I stopped putting them in the laundry basket for fear she'd throw them away. "For heaven's sake let me wash them," she said. Reluctantly, I gave them to her to wash and she did a terrible thing; she ripped the zipper out. She'd yelled and lectured me in the past but she never committed such a violent act. I was furious. I wouldn't wear the new shorts she made me. I wore jeans in the heat of summer and pouted.

She must have felt a little bad because she didn't put the shorts in the rag bag to use for dusting and polishing. She threw them out so neither of us would have to confront them again. In that way she felt that I couldn't hold a grudge and she wouldn't have to feel guilty. Ha!

~

You must have had an article of clothing that you were inordinately fond of? Something that made you feel like a princess or an outlaw or an artist or a just a "player?"

I knew a woman who had her own personal clothing museum. In a tiny attic she displayed the dress she met her husband in, the shoes she wore to a Grateful Dead concert in 1971, a hat she wore all through Mexico searching for Dog Girls, her baby shoes, a ripped Girl Scout uniform painted with skulls and coffins that she'd worn to a Halloween party in 1985, and various other pieces with impressive provenance.

~

Aside from the plaid shorts and a few gifts, M made all my clothes, even when I was in college. She was an excellent seamstress and knitter. I got to pick out patterns and material every year before school started. She did occasionally veto my choices and I could never make her understand why some things were cool and others were definitely NOT. Sometimes she'd change a collar or length on me; sometimes, despite both our best efforts at design, they'd turn out horrible. But I'd wear them once or twice even if I hated them because she worked so hard making them.

When they turned out good, they were awesome: one-of-a-kind, latest trend, perfect fit—nothing better. I was shocked when I started buying store-bought clothes to find out how much I'd have to spend to duplicate my mother's perfection.

In memoriam: the plaid Bermuda shorts, RIP. The full "Mexican-print" skirt I wore the first day of fourth grade, ole! The balloon dress. The sac dress (for comic relief). The Moose sweater. The black floral bell-bottoms I wore all through college. The brown and white poncho (cotton, not scratchy wool) she knitted for me. The red sundress made of vintage 30's fabric. The velvet jacket that my daughter still wears even though it's older than she is.

Hours of sewing, hours of knitting, thank you M.

~

I buried my mother in a store-bought dress.

It was lilac and purchased for her Fiftieth Anniversary. I made a small party for the occasion at a restaurant in my hometown; she said it was the best night of her life. Since my parents had gotten married at the courthouse without fanfare, I told the local baker to make them a real wedding cake because "they never had a wedding." My mother was horrified that he'd think they weren't really married. She told him the whole story about going to the Justice of the Peace in a blue suit she made herself and borrowed shoes, my dad in his Navy uniform.

He didn't care.

~

I don't include underwear in my memorial. It's not that I'm embarrassed, just practical, a straight cotton kinda gal. I do own a pink lacy pair of tap pants and satin camisole and have bought various thongs, push-up bras that don't work unless you have something to push up, and a Merry Widow (Oh my god! Did they really sneak girdles back on us!) I have worn garter belts, but only because I was born before pantyhose.

It's my hope that if something happens to me, it won't happen at the end of the week because that's when I'm relegated to wearing my "old lady" underwear. I've promised myself to buy new underwear but I never seem to get around to it. The last time I did, was when I realized that three pair of my "good" underpants had all but disintegrated. The "old lady" underwear is nearly indestructible.

Socks, on the other hand, are alive. They can be as expressive and as anonymous as you prefer. But don't cross them; they aren't as inanimate as you think. They don't like the laundry even though they're ideal candidates for frequent washings. They tend to hide in pillowcases and often run away. Their sensitivity is understandable; how would you like getting stepped on all the time.

For a long time, I kept the socks I was wearing when my daughter was born. I barely made it to the hospital and didn't get completely undressed in time for the birth. When they wheeled me into the hospital, Louis saw two guys he did business with. "Wave to Mac and Sydney," he said. "I have to sell them next week." Luckily for him, I had a massive contraction just then and was unable to slug him.

My white knee socks stayed miraculously clean through the whole ordeal. I don't know why she was in such a hurry.

~

Some day they'll have a funeral for Smiggle's Bottom. I've had it in my mind lately. Not much left of the town now, there was only a crossroad to begin with. The railroad station was torn down and the tracks have weeds growing through them. Most of the railroad bridges have fallen and the ones that remain hang precariously. Some of the people who live there have gone crazy. Crazy was always rampant as few loonies were ever "put away;" they were left to roam about or sit in their childhood homes until parents and relatives died and they became part of the local vegetation.

Boo Buchholz lived in a shack on the mountain near Wisdom Killbridge's farm. Wisdom and Mona Killbridge were friends of my grandmother and we often went for visits. Boo Buchholz would sneak up on us and say, you guessed it, "Boo." He was an old man when I was a little girl and by the time I was eleven or twelve, he seemed to have disappeared. Mrs. Killbridge said, "Oh, old Boo never comes out anymore. The welfare worker checks in once in a while and the Baptists bring him food every now and again. I take him a plate sometimes. When I do, I call out from the fence and he gets dressed and puts on his hat to greet me but he never steps out of the doorway."

When my dad died, Ray Clark came to the funeral home. He'd bought the Killbridge farm after they died and was eking a living out growing corn and marijuana. I asked him about Boo.

"You have to see it to believe it," he said. "Old Boo turned into a tree, an honest-to-God Ash tree. I know you don't want to believe it. Come on up and see for yourself."

After the funeral my son stayed to help me clean out the house. We took Louis and Paige (my daughter) to the airport, stopped to get something to eat on the way back and got lost. When I saw the road to Jack's Run I proposed a side trip and Harlie said he didn't care. So we went up Six Mile Hill.

It was summer and still light. I didn't bother to stop at Ray Clark's house though he probably knew I was there since there aren't many cars that come up that way and pot growers are pretty vigilant.

The old shanty was collapsing into the field and, sure enough, a gnarly Ash tree was growing up out of one side, as ugly a tree as I'd ever seen. I walked close and studied the bark; there were some old rags hanging off it and something eerily familiar. It was nearly leafless even though it was early September, still summer. I thought I heard something and looked around to see if it was Harlie, but he was leaning up against the car, looking at his shoes.

It could have been the wind blowing through the old trees, or Ray Clark playing a trick and Harlie was too deep in thoughtfulness and grief to hear it. But it did sound like someone whispering, "Boo."

~

It's a weird thing about crazy. Some people can tell you they hear voices and talk to dead people and they're not considered crazy at all; in fact, those kind of talents can make a person pretty successful. In some places these people are called Shamans and they're important people in tribal cultures. In our town we had a lot of them and they were taken for granted. We had a whole class of them at school; it was called "the special class." When the Special Kids got tired of school, they roamed around or sat at home. You mostly couldn't tell them from "normal" people in our part of the world. They only got "put away" if they were violent. If they had no kin, neighbors looked after them.

Mr. Shultz got put away because he beat his wife and wouldn't let her out of the house for two years. She signed him out of the loony bin and he went after the welfare worker with a knife so the state put him away for good.

Annie Oakley and I had a common interest in cowboys. Everyone played dead when she shot them with her toy gun. She was a lot of fun.

Mookie Purrier would ask you baseball scores in the middle of winter and football scores in July. I have to admit that I didn't know why this was considered crazy for a long time—I'm not much of a sports fan. You could make up any score or story for him, "the Hunker Headcases beat the Paris Periopolos by twelve," and he'd hoot and holler, jump around and sing to you.

Amlan Ray was my idol though. She was a Shaman for

sure. Amlan would stand in the middle of 119 (the biggest highway near our town). She always had her accordion and an old cup. Cars would whiz by her and she'd play and sing her heart out till Sheriff Harden came and took her home. I watched from a monkey ball tree on the hill above. I spent a lot of time in that old monkey ball tree, daydreaming and watching cars. What she was doing was collecting foreign wind from those cars, breezes from West Virginia and Ocean City Maryland, maybe from  as far away as Nashville or New Orleans.

She knew I was up in that tree watching because every once in a while she'd turn around and look. She never offered me a cup of the foreign wind though, it was her prize. I'd have to get out of town by mustering up my own magic.

One day I found her accordion by the side of the road. She just disappeared. She released all that foreign wind and let it blow her away; that's what I think.

It's not what Sheriff Harden thinks.

~

Lately, Louis hears voices. "What?" he says. "What did you say?" He thinks it's me when I haven't said a word. We don't know who's talking to him or what they're trying to tell him.

~

IT MAY NOT SEEM LIKE IT, BUT I MAKE VERY GOOD USE
OF MY TIME BY DAYDREAMING AND MAKING THINGS UP.
I MADE YOU UP. THINK ABOUT IT

~

Here's the part about ghosts: It's true that my mother died on my birthday. That day's only a couple of weeks after Mother's Day, which is the last time I saw her. Now, every year she comes back for the two weeks between Mother's Day and my birthday, and plays tricks on me. She hides things; she makes the appointments that are marked on the calendar disappear and reappear after I've missed them; she changes the time. She makes me get on the wrong train. She loses my place in books, sometimes she loses the whole book. She makes rings fall off my fingers into pocketbooks, and laundry where I find them weeks later.

She turns into the coyote trickster, something I think she always wanted to be but was too timid to try. It's been so many years now and I know not to take on anything monumental at that time of year because she'll turn it inside-out. I just sit back and enjoy the ride.

I'm glad she's having fun; she deserves it. And I'm glad we can still laugh together.

One year she had me convinced she'd come back as a dog. I was walking down the street in New York City and this big mutt rounded the corner (with her person in tow), ran up, and jumped on me. I wasn't shocked or frightened because I recognized her. It didn't bother me a bit. The dog's person was horrified and apologetic. "Don't worry," I told him. "We know each other from another life." It was obvious that the dog and I recognized each other but her person didn't know what to think.

Something about that dog's eyes reminded me of my mother. I never had a moment of doubt. I had the urge to offer the man anything for the dog; I wanted my mother back. Then I realized what the date was. "You almost got me this time," I told the dog.

When he got the dog off me, the man hurried away. No one in my hometown would have acted that way. They would have accepted my story or at least humored me.

~

My dad is not so frivolous. He doesn't play tricks from beyond the grave; he's happy to finally be with my mother again. Having been a magician, doing tricks all his life, he may be tricked out. Then again, he wasn't frivolous about his magic tricks. He practiced all the time—when he wasn't at work (and sometimes when he was). After dinner he'd sit with his lap-desk and practice card tricks for hours. He took good care of his cards too; he powdered them and did something with Elmer's Glue to preserve them. He always carried a deck of cards with him, even to the next world.

Magic is a serious thing, not to be taken lightly. It has to be practiced and done in the right frame of mind. Any magician or Shaman will tell you that. Some people are born with that frame of mind, like Amlan. And some people have to work hard at their magic, like my dad.

I just wait for it to come my way—and it does come every now-and-again.

If you live in a big city, you can only tell certain people about the magic that comes your way. Never tell your boss or your mother-in-law unless you know they won't freak out.

~

Sometimes when a Shaman dies, his or her magic is passed on.

I have a different kind of magic than my dad. My magic doesn't show in front of people often; only special ones have seen it.

# Chapter 12

## God and Men

It's very important to have a proper funeral. There are no rules for "proper," but some thought and appropriate ritual should go into it. People who go to "shrinks" and read self-help books call this "closure" for the survivors. I suppose this is a good word but sometimes things don't stay closed, like in the case of my mother. I wouldn't want her to be "closed;" it's comforting to know she's still around.

I prefer the idea of "send off." You can't let anything go unless you give it some sort of send off.

For instance, when John Lennon was killed a whole generation—and a lot of others—went into mourning. People I hadn't heard from since college called me to commiserate. Old friendships were rekindled; new friendships were cemented. My four-year-old daughter came home every day and listened to the *Double Fantasy* album and watched the cartoon version of *Yellow Submarine*.

After a few days, I heard her and my son arguing.

"But he's still on the record; he's still in the movie," she insisted.

"That's different," my son yelled back. "He's dead and dead means gone!"

How do you explain death to a child when you don't understand it yourself?

It seemed as if Yoko wouldn't have a funeral, and you can't blame her. Many of John's fans had been unkind to her in the past and now she had reason to fear for her and her sons' lives. But the world camped out at her doorstep.

She finally consented to a memorial in Central Park. We watched thousands of people gather in the park from the roof of our building. We listened and watched it on TV. There were songs and speeches and moments of silence—that everyone in the world could observe. The silence of such a large group of people is monumental.

Afterward, the crowds dispersed; a bit of sun came out and my daughter went back to listening to *Really Rosie*.

Though the dead often seem to be very much with us, their official send off is important if you're to go on with your life.

My cousin Nadine went to Memphis when Elvis died. She stood at the gates of Graceland with a multitude of other fans. They talked and wept. I suppose they sang and listened to music—the Lennon fans did. Nadine hasn't had a pleasant life. Two husbands left her and her children are not well; one is a drug addict. Nadine is plagued with health problems and can't bring herself to stop smoking though she knows it'll kill her. Some days Nadine can't get out of bed because she's in such pain from arthritis and emphysema. But most days she paints her face, puts on enough jewelry to impress a Rap star, and hobbles off to work humming Elvis' songs.

Her only social activity is a meeting every other month in Trotter, Georgia with a small Elvis fan club. Some of these people play instruments; the rest dance. The music is not necessarily Elvis'. They drink Jack Daniels and Kool Aid, and eat a different thing every month. After a hurricane once, they took fried peanut butter and banana sandwiches to victims, "as Elvis would have done."

These are people Nadine met at the gates of Graceland when Elvis died. There are probably other such groups. Nadine says that Elvis had a grand send off; it was certainly the high point of her life.

I knew a girl who stole her dad's car and drove to Washington, D.C. for President Kennedy's funeral. We were in high school when he died. It was a great shock to the world as well as high school kids, who heard it in class when the principal relayed a radio station through the PA system without a word of warning. His and Oswald's deaths were the first deaths we watched again and again on TV.

I wasn't particularly interested in political leaders at that time. The Kennedys were glamorous but I was much more interested in the fanciful and humorous. I did feel bad for Jackie and her children. And I was not pleased afterward to be stuck with Lyndon Johnson, who was even less fanciful and humorous than Kennedy.

There were plenty of people in my town who were overwrought at Kennedy's death, especially Catholics who have a wonderful sense of ritual. Those were the days of Latin masses. I loved going to church with Catholic friends: stand up, sit down, kneel—rocking from knees to seat and back, the strange language, incense smoke wafting through the church, the huddling of ladies-in-black, scarves.

Still, the Kennedy send off was a little much—though not as much as poor Princess Diana. Don't get me started.

~

## Religion

I've mentioned the religions of my grandparents, though only Gram Little was very serious about it. My parents were not very religious. Pop taught me that there was one God (I'm not so sure about that now) and that everyone believed in Him (!!!); they just went about worshiping "Him" in different ways. It didn't matter where you went or how you went about worshiping as long as you didn't intentionally hurt anyone and tried to be a good person. It was that simple for my dad.

My parents went to whatever church was in the neighborhood or with any friends that asked them. My dad went to various Protestant churches, Catholic masses, and temple with Jewish friends. I was encouraged to go to as many different services as I wished, but not encouraged to "join up" until I was older. All in all, it's a pretty good way of looking at religion, if you ask me.

I have expanded beyond this view to an appreciation of all forms of spirituality. I've amassed a system of beliefs that have elements of the Judeo-Christian as well as Taoist, Buddhist, Islam, Pagan, and various smaller sects. The only beliefs I disdain are extremisms. Beliefs that are nurturing and ethical are all "good medicine." Those that are extreme and restrictive only cause trouble in the world.

~

For several of my teen years I attended the Sunday night Mustard Street Methodist Youth Group. This wasn't because of any affinity for Methodist beliefs. In fact, I was unable, then or now, to discern any major differences between Protestant denominations. My interest was purely sexual and centered on Johnny Stange. I was thirteen; he was fifteen and came from far enough away that he went to a different school. This made him practically foreign. Had he gone to school with me, I probably would've fainted dead away in the stairwell or been unable to sit upright in my seat. As it was, I was too shy to talk to him unless imposed upon by religious necessity—like carrying garbage from pancake breakfasts, or hiding Easter eggs for Sunday school children.

Johnny Stange didn't know it was the sixties. He still wore his hair in a DA with a perfect curl that came down over his forehead. He wore what looked like a bathtub chain around his neck and pants that incited the imagination. Outside the Mustard Street MYG he was most likely a hood whose mother dumped him off every Sunday night in the hope of saving him. He was not well-behaved at MYG but his vulnerability showed up every once in a while. God, how I love a guy with a little outlaw in him. I wanted to save Johnny Stange myself.

Other girls thought he was icky but he was the star of my fantasies for more than a year. Then the Methodists got serious about confirming us and I backed out quietly.

Because he didn't live in our town, I never saw him on the street or at local hangouts—not that I was any kind of regular at "hangouts." I was seventeen, just before graduation, when I pulled my dad's car into a gas station and was greeted by Johnny Stange. He flashed me a flirtatious smile (was it just my imagination?), but gave no indication that he recognized me. He couldn't have been embarrassed because gas station attendant was a well respected occupation in our town; it was the measure of my invisibility, a quality I'd carefully cultivated. He still had the hair and looked terrific in his gas station jumpsuit. He "fucked" my fantasies for weeks after, fantasies that helped me subdue my anxiety about going off to college. I had a plan. If college didn't work out, I'd come back and fall into the arms of Johnny Stange. I might consent to a Methodist wedding but we would live a life of Buddhist Pagan Taoist bliss in the mountains above Smiggle's Bottom.

~

Later, when college got to be too much, I'd remember Johnny Stange and think about getting stuck in Smiggle's Bottom with him. Johnny probably thought a Buddhist was some kind of foreign car.

So much for religion.

# Chapter 13

## Family Legends

Family legends are a lot of what you hear at funerals. Every family has them, some more fanciful than others. The families of many of my current friends have legends about great wealth and power, American founding fathers or brave escapes from other countries. This is not true in either of my parent's families, with one exception: Gabe.

I'm not sure how Gabe was related to me, perhaps he was one of those cousins of my cousins, but he was something to Gram Little because the aunts told me his story at her 100th Birthday (sort of a pre-funeral that the person can enjoy while still alive, with cake and their name mentioned on *The Today Show*).

Gabe was what they call an "Idiot Savant." This was very common in Gram Little's family; there were great-uncles that couldn't spell their name but guessed the jelly beans in the jar at Kunkle's store every year. No one ever took a music lesson but I had cousins that could play Rockabilly on six instruments.

Gabe had no obvious "idiot" traits; he just wasn't very good at school. Each year they "contemplated holding him back," but having been "held back" twice, his size was beginning to frighten the other children.

At home Gabe took apart every electrical appliance he could get his hands on. From the time he was five, every gadget he put back together worked better than it had before he fiddled with it. The toaster had a smoke alarm when a piece of toast was about to burn. He added speakers to the radio to make it "close to stereo" before anyone had even heard the word "stereo." The toilet cleaned itself; you just had to add half a cup of Bactine to an attached mechanism once a month. The six year old Plymouth could cruise at 190 mph. And, best of all, he did something to their black and white TV in 1953, that made the picture appear to be in color! (Maybe not realistic colors, but silver and India red, strawberry and indigo.)

No one knows how he accomplished these miraculous feats but Uncle Asa took a hair-raising ride in the car and Cherrilyn (who is somebody's cousin) saw the TV and swore to the colors.

One day, so it goes, two strange men in black suits came to Gabe's house. His mother thought for sure they were there to cart him off to Juvy, but they turned out to be big industrialists who'd heard of Gabe. Now this is the part that's hard to believe. I can see the toaster, the radio, the car, even the toilet and TV. But how did two "big industrialists" hear about some retard in Kilmer, West Virginia? In 1955! This frightens me. It's as strange as the dissection of aliens in Rosedale, or Roseville, or whatever that place is.

Gabe hadn't graduated from high school, but these guys hired him on the spot. (I presume they tested the augmented appliances.) They took him to California, which was as remote as Tibet for our family. The industrialists ensconced him in a fully fitted laboratory, offered him any materials he might need, and gave him free reign to do what he wanted. He only worked for them a few years and the government stepped in. He told his mother he'd be working in an undisclosed place on secret projects so she couldn't get in touch with him, not that she'd been in touch with him very much while he was in California (remember the family aversion to long distance phone calls and airplanes).

When his father died, she dialed a number he'd given her
and he showed up two weeks after the funeral to spend the day
with her. He had with him a device he'd invented, something
like a phone, she said. But without any wires and he could use
it to call anywhere in the world. This was 1959, long before
anyone ever dreamed of anything like the cell phone. Needless
to say, when the cell phone finally came about, my relatives
claimed the inventor, the real inventor, was one of their own.

No one has ever heard from Gabe since, not even when his
own mother died.

~

Gram Little told Cora and me a story after Aunt Kat's first
husband's funeral that's stranger than legend. It doesn't seem
that she told it to anyone else and I don't know why she chose
us, but this is it: Some time after her first five children were
born and they were living on the Poor farm (Poor being the
name of the landlord of the farm, remember?), she had a
horrendous accident. She was sweeping the porch and lost her
balance, the railing gave way and she "fell on the broom." I
don't remember exactly how she described it; Gram Little was
beyond timid about some things. She was in her nineties when
she told us this and she was perfectly sincere and though she
was not entirely clear, we knew it was something we shouldn't
ask too many details about.

She called her sons and told them to run out to the field
and get Pa. Her husband put her in a wagon and drove her into
town. The doctor then "sewed her shut."

How do you question a ninety-six-year-old woman about
a story like that? You're in such shock that all you can do is
sit and listen. You don't dare ask for details. Ugh! You wonder

afterward if you'd heard what you thought you'd heard. When I asked Cora about it later, she said, "Did she really say that? What do you suppose really happened?" Neither one of us could imagine.

Gram believed that she would never have any more children after that, but a miracle happened. Four years later my mother was born, and after her, three more children. I have always questioned the story of "virgin" births and was too cowardly to ask the nature of this particular "miracle."

I've often pondered what the truth of this story could possibly be. I haven't any idea why Gram Little would decide to tell such a story and never had the nerve to bring it up again.

~

My grandmothers both had all their children at home. One of my Manx grandmother's babies weighed over nine pounds, the other weighed over ten. Ouch!

~

Injun' Al is the oldest of Gram Little's family legends. It's not clear whether he was an Indian (Native American) or he married an Indian and people called him names because of it. (Those were times before "political correctness," and high times for bullying.) If we could prove anything about him, we would all have gotten college tuition from the government or, at least, jobs in casinos. Alas, Injun' Al was disowned by family and society; his children, apparently embarrassed by their heritage, successfully concealed traces of his and his wife's existence.

It's said he was Seneca. This is possible because there were some Senecas in what is now Ohio, close to where the Little family settled.

The Seneca's name in their own language is Ogwenoweh and means "Great Hill People." My grandfather's family, the Littles, were small valley people so Al must have been from Gram's side (the Moore's).

In the Seneca myth of Creation, the earth is covered with water and birds spread their wings to save a woman who fell from Heaven. They place her on a giant tortoise which expands to become an island and then expands further to become all the land masses of the planet. The woman gives birth to twins, a Good Spirit and an Evil Spirit. Here's the part I like: eventually the Sky Holder decides to populate the earth with humans and sends six pairs, which become various tribes.

I love the idea of a Sky Holder, and can certainly identify with a woman who falls from the Heavens. This may be why my mother dreamt of flying.

The Seneca's also have a dragon, called Anguid. I'm fond of dragons and happy to hear that the Americas might have had some and that I might have had an ancestor who killed one, like St. George. I hope he didn't kill the last one.

~

My father wasn't interested in legends. He did not dream of being descended from Indians or Gypsies or apes or stars. He wasn't even proud of the possibility that he might have been a descendent of Vikings, which he probably was as the only time the Isle of Man was conquered by another culture was the 400 years it was under the rule of Vikings.

My father and Manx grandmother were both red-headed

and Nordic looking. Pop loved the idea of the sea, though after crossing it twice when he was a child, he never saw it again. He joined the Navy, but was stationed in Cleveland.

I was enthralled with Kirk Douglas in the movie "The Vikings." I saw it five times the year it came out and have seen it several times on television since. Each time I hope that he'll beat out Tony Curtis for the love of Janet Leigh. I don't know how Janet Leigh could possibly go for the Tony Curtis character when she was loved by Kirk Douglas. After I saw the movie I performed several Viking funerals for pets (in local creeks). I still cry when they send Kirk Douglas off in the flaming boat.

Hail Ragnor!

# Chapter 14

## How I'm Related to the People in my Neighborhood Now

Homage

I admire the way she can wear at least three dresses, even in the heat of summer, the way she paints her hair and fingernails in bright colors with magic markers. I admire the way her head hangs buoyantly when she sleeps on the stoop across the street, multicolored snarls in the capacity of dream antenna. I envy the collection of mysterious treasures she keeps in bags attached to an old stroller, never letting them out of her sight. She has her own style and the dust of ages to validate it, dust she wears proudly and refuses to wash off. She never wavers from life in the street, yet isn't seduced by trends. Not one to incur reality from TV; she surrounds herself with it.

She has an excellent memory: "You wore that shirt two days ago," she yells at me; "You've been wearing those pants for years. Buy a new pair already." She's undoubtedly right, for my own memory is less than trustworthy. I can't remember where my shoes are or which block the bank is on. For this reason, I make things up as I go along and would wear the same clothes over and over if it were not for her. I don't mind having to invent a reality; it's better than letting someone else do it.

I was drawn to her at first by her humming; she makes a beautiful sound while inventorying and rearranging her treasures. Her voice resonates like a low pipe. It reminds me of my childhood, most of which is lost along with the TV remote and my red jacket. Tomorrow I'll spend the morning cooking and when she's sleeping, I'll leave three buttery scones and a package of new magic markers at her feet.

Could I have invented a creature so grand?

~

Someday I'll look out my window and she'll have disappeared. Am I the only one who'll miss her?

~

I expect to see him crouched beneath the bridge as I pass by on my inspection round, but there are only the coded marks left by "**Doze**" and "**LLOW**," "**CL**" and "**Stain**." I follow the echo of his ravings as they bounce from building to building about me; he's not harassing people in Dunkin' Donuts, passed out among the debris between buildings, panhandling Alfredo's Pizza customers, communing with the Rum Phantoms on the corner, conning the barman at Shade's Saloon, or afoot anywhere in the neighborhood. He may have been picked up by the cops, or worse, the Salvies. He may have been called in... or he might have gone to the Gospel Father's soup kitchen, but not at this hour.

Or perhaps he's taken a government mission, or found a position with some creative company soliciting outsider theories. He may have found a small apartment in a well-kept walk-up; he could be carrying paint cans and drop cloths, wearing a Gap T-shirt and new Nikes, prospering.

He might have decomposed into cosmic particles...But no, a pigeon is delicately sipping at a pool of fresh vomit, undoubtedly his at this time of day. He's been here recently and may still be nearby, indifferent to my agitation, amused by my perplexity, unaware of my concern.

~

These are people who deserve a Viking funeral. Who will do it for them?

~~

For most people, death is experienced as a loss, but this is not so for everyone. Some people only think about what they stand to accumulate, how much of the dead person's possessions will become theirs.

Mrs. DeMontagnac had two nieces that she supported from childhood. Her sister and brother-in-law were were solidly middle class or would have been if they had been less frivolous with their spending. Mrs. DeMontagnac had the means and the will to indulge their children. Her own daughter was inclined to be plain and unassuming. As a child she was happy with pots and pans, crayons and paper. She grew up insisting on living her own life and was content to work and earn a living. So when her nieces were born, Mrs. DeMontagnac bought them cashmere swaddling blankets (her daughter was allergic to wool of any kind), Princess rocking horses with side saddles, and Bugatti tricycles, all the things her daughter had rejected.

Encouraged by their parents, the nieces became insatiable. They wanted everything they saw or heard about: Steiff bears, Chanel outfits for their Barbies, a playhouse in the form of the Chateau de Talcy. The older they got, the more their demands multiplied. When they were in their twenties, they began to use Mrs. DeMontagnac's credit cards for online purchases. They learned how to access her checking account. They took cash from her pocketbook and refused to work because, they said, "Auntie promised us the good life." They insisted that she owed them for all the things they did for her. In truth, they only went to her home in order to steal. Always in new clothes, jewelry and pocketbooks, they were walking billboards of larceny in wardrobes with logos: alligators, polo ponies, flags; clothing and accessories decorated with initials that weren't theirs: DK, YL, D & G, LV. Their hair was dyed, their faces painted, and their butts declared them "Juicy!" Despite all the finery, they'd never meet the men they adored: Giorgio, Calvin, Ralph, Marc.

Mrs. DeMontagnac's friends and daughter tried to step in but Mrs. DeMontagnac couldn't bring herself to prosecute them or cut them off entirely because she didn't want to disturb her sister, their mother, who had become very ill. Mrs. DeMontagnac, who was quite a bit older than her sister, wasn't well either. The girls demoralized her. That, and the stress of her sister's illness, finally killed Mrs. DeMontagnac.

The nieces expected to take possession of everything she'd owned. They went to her house the day she died to collect her clothes, jewelry and shoes (she'd been very well dressed). But Mrs. DeMontagnac's daughter, grandchildren, two other sisters, and friends decided to honor her will and distribute what assets she had left, fairly. They found that her finances had been mismanaged and drained. Her home had been neglected for years and was worth very little. The fine silver and china she collected during her lifetime was missing as was her good jewelry, expensive designer clothes, and pocketbooks. Her collection of Hummel and Lladro figurines was gone and the six early Goya lithographs that hung in her dining room had been replaced with museum posters. There was barely enough to bury her and pay off debts and lawyer fees. Her daughter decided to spend what little there was, on her funeral. The nieces whined and ranted. They claimed that they were entitled to Mrs. DeMontagnac's fortune. They expected to become rich. They accused her daughter of cheating them, but it was no secret that they were the ones who'd done the cheating and theft. Everyone who'd come in contact with Mrs. DeMonagnac in the last twenty years of her life, knew the stories.

No one who behaves in such a manner is entitled to anything but scorn. Luckily, it's not up to us to bestow this. Karma comes back in its own way. One of the nieces lived a good life until her breast implants exploded and the bodies of eleven ex-husbands were found in her back yard. The other ended up in a cardboard box outside of Powerline, Kentucky with a one-armed, virus-infected Steiff bear as companion.

~~~

How did I meet Ida Wineberg?

I decided to sneak into an adult class at a local university. I'd reached an age when I was seldom questioned by younger people. Growing old is not the terrible experience it's been made out to be. I'm able to get away with a lot, and expect the possibilities to multiply in relation to my increasing grey hair and wrinkles.

This particular class was quite small and when we were introducing ourselves, the teacher became confused about the fact that I was not "on the list." She speculated that I might have been lost in the computer.

"I don't feel lost," I whispered to Ida, who I didn't know at the time. The idea of being lost in a computer had never entered my mind. I saw a movie once where a boy was sucked into a computer and became a sort of cartoon figure in cyberspace. The teacher looked so disturbed that I thought she might be thinking something similar. She was such a nice woman that I promised to check in with the office after class.

There was a young man in the class that introduced himself by commenting on the fact that his generation was largely phony: phony hair color, phony tribal markings, phony enthusiasms. He wanted to take a class populated by older, more genuine people. It was a shocking confession. How do young people become genuine unless they try out various illusory personas? I continue to experiment and don't consider it unscrupulous to do so.

Ida, who was in her late seventies (or beyond) at the time, was next to introduce herself. "My name is Ida Wineberg," she said. "My hair is not genuine, my eyesight has been augmented, and my shoes and pocketbook are copies of more expensive brands. My teeth are false. I was not born in this country and the broach I'm wearing is made of paste and glass."

I was immediately drawn to Ida and she went with me the next day to enroll in the class legally. Officially, the class was full but two older women can talk young people into bending rules rather easily.

Ida escaped from Vienna a moment before the Nazis entered. She was sixteen and no one else in her family was spared. She was taken to Israel first and later immigrated to the United States.

Ida is a comical cynic. She doesn't dwell on the tragedy of her past; she doesn't harp on the holocaust. She believes that the world is filled with chaos and paradox, and refuses to waste her time trying to understand or explain it. She says that she's too occupied with the business of surviving from day to day.

She reads comic books. She drinks espresso and eats rich pastries from a Viennese shop on East Tenth Street. She puts chocolate on everything. She keeps a dream journal but embellishes the dreams. She walks with a cane, not because she's dependent on it, but because she likes to walk in the city at night and might find occasion to use it for protection. She has a son that moved his family to Israel, but she won't give up her New York City life to be near them.

The stories she tells about the time before the war are chilling. The Austrian Jews were in jeopardy long before the Nazis marched in. She says she's seen atrocities occur in many other places during her lifetime; she recognizes that atrocities are happening now, even here. She says this is the way of humanity.

She doesn't fear death; she still finds reasons to laugh.

~

You always worry about friends that are older. Some of them worry and complain; others don't worry at all. There's absolutely no advantage to worrying, but it's an inescapable habit. The same thing can be said of pity; pity is the lowest emotion. It does no one any good and can be humiliating. The lowest of the low is self-pity.

# Chapter 15

## Bedtime Stories and Other Customs

*?Greenwood Heights?* ~~

There was an old woman who lived in a house down the alley from Linden Hill Apartments. Late one afternoon in early winter, just before twilight, I was coming home and saw her on the porch. She had wild grey hair like antennas and a lumpy body that may not have been human. She never said anything but looked at you like she knew something terrible that you didn't. I hid in the bushes, waiting for her to go in before I walked by. It was getting colder, beginning to snow and she had no coat on.

She stood there watching snow flakes for a while, then I thought I saw her feet leave the ground. Did I really see a sliver of winter light between her worn boot and the porch boards? I stepped out from behind the bushes and inched closer. Wind blew the snow beneath her into a cloud of camouflage. I moved closer. Her eyes were closed. She was rising. Up. Up, into the bright winter sky, the silvery snow twinkled about her. Her skirts billowed with swirling the snow.

No one else saw...

~~

Once there was a quiet little girl who had a quiet little family in a quiet little town, on (what else?) a quiet little street. She was not

131

a very neat little girl; her hands were dirty, her pants too big, and her hair too short to hide the cowlicks. This little girl wanted, more than anything, to have some noise in her life, something big and loud and frightening. She wanted chaos and magic, a dragon, an earthquake, a volcano eruption on Ash Street. She wanted electric guitars and fire and the kind of floats that were in the Macy's Thanksgiving parade.

The girl's mother wanted her to do her arithmetic homework. It was the girl's worst subject. She didn't understand the monumental significance that people gave to numbers. She could see very little use for them. Her teacher, Miss Bell, thought numbers were magic. The little girl thought Miss Bell was boring in her beige blouses and practical shoes. "Arithmetic, yuck!" the girl said. "It's worse than spelling. A Rat In The House May Eat The Ice Cream."

Her father wanted her to clean her room and go to sleep. The little girl wanted to go out into the moonlight and dance in her grass skirt. "It's too cold," her mother said. "It's too late," her father said. "You'll wake the baby." (The baby lived three houses away!)

"Where's your schoolwork?"

"A dragon ate it."

"What are we going to do with her?"

They decided to let her wear the blue pajamas with clouds and stars on them and do the arithmetic under her bed with a flashlight where she fell asleep.

Her mother decided not to disturb her since the girl had finished her arithmetic. The little girl dreamed that numbers were flying around her room like big flat insects. They dive-bombed her bed and toy box looking for her but couldn't find her under the bed. Toward morning there was a terrible storm that woke the girl up. Rain beat at the windows; wind howled and threw branches off trees; thunder and lightening came so rapidly that you couldn't count even one-one-thousand between them. The little house shivered. In the morning the world was transformed. What had seemed quietly angry was now brightly colored or oddly crooked and raving. Sounds came out of the little houses, Beatles music, Jimi Hendrix. Flowers sang harmony and the old trees chanted; the grass sang back-up. Clouds screeched to a halt overhead, then took off with a squeal; traffic on the roads multiplied.

Older small-towners were horrified and the children loved it.

But this is a fairytale and the children grew up. The chaos got out of hand and some of the grown-up children took advantage. The earth itself was unhappy and began to rumble and erupt in anger. People blamed each other.

The scariest thing about it was it wasn't the end of the world.

~~

Louis' Uncle Sy was not a pleasant man to be around. At family gatherings he drank too much, slobbered and spit into his food. His wife was fat and unpleasant. They bickered constantly and though they didn't do anything purposefully offensive to others, it was uncomfortable to be around them. I didn't ever have one meaningful conversation with him (and I'm a person who's learned something from just about everyone I ever met). I never heard him say a kind word to his wife or their son.

When our children were young, we hired a babysitter once a week and went to a restaurant for dinner. One night we went to a place in Chelsea. It was before the neighborhood was gentrified and the restaurant wasn't fancy, but the food was decent. We sat in the back and talked quietly; couples with young children rarely get a chance to talk to each other uninterrupted or when they're not totally exhausted.

We were ready to leave when Uncle Sy came in—with a strange woman. She was not an attractive woman and it wasn't the sort of place you'd take a hooker. Who could believe that anyone would want to go out with Sy, to eat with him in public! What could the attraction possibly be?

"Let's get out of here," I whispered.

"How can we? We'd have to walk right by him."

"Isn't that **his** problem?"

"I can't do it. Eat some dessert. Have another drink."

When he died, I was happy we hadn't left the restaurant. His wife and grown son looked so lost. They didn't cry; they just stared at the casket and the family with a look of subdued desperation and loss.

It's amazing what people can miss.

~

The death of a loving parent (friend, relative, co-worker) is sometimes easier than the death of one with whom issues remain unresolved.

Don't repress your emotions; they'll eat away at you long after the culprit is gone.

~

Louis' Aunt Abby was loved by all. When her quiet husband, David, died everyone gathered at her house to sit *shiva*. Uncle David had been sick for a long time, suffering a slow deterioration that made it harder and harder to move, to breathe. He'd been in a coma for weeks. Aunt Abby had always been a "take charge" kind of woman. She fawned over Uncle David and ordered doctors and nurses around during his sickness.

Abby spend the first few days of *shiva* sitting on a box in the corner, not eating anything. Word went out that reinforcements were needed; friends and relatives rallied to her side. While men talked sports in whispers, the women cooked and gossiped. Aunt Abby was moved to a kitchen chair and fortified with endless cups of tea and spoonfuls of each dish. "Taste the brisket, Abby." "Is there too much sugar in the Kugel, Abby?" "You must taste Mrs. Gambino's veal parmesan."

Soon Aunt Abby was directing meals and packaging leftovers for the faithful. The purpose of sitting *shiva* is to keep the grievers busy until the initial shock of death has passed. It worked for Abby.

Within a year she moved to Boca with a cousin and has taken up golf.

While the men play games of skill, the women are left to cook and gossip. Their laughter infuses the sauce of gemfruit and mountain herb. The meat of the red phoenix is handled with respect and clean hands. It is carefully prepared, marinated in the finest herbs, wrapped in leaves of the memoria tree, and placed in a newly dug cooking pit. The dogs appear to be asleep but are actually watching the food preparation with great interest. Old men sit on the beach smoking pipes of ien, remembering bygone exploits, which may or may not have occurred.

~~

If you walked down the alley from Linden Hill Apartments, going toward the river, you came to the Lord Baby Jesus Baptist Church. Until I was fourteen, this was just a cinder-block foundation; the church wasn't actually raised until the summer of 1960. Because the summers in our valley were hot and windless, and because there was no air conditioning, the LBJBC left its doors and windows open. The music that came from this unfinished church was magical. After a long day of riding bikes and building hide-outs, we kids would sit on the fence across the dirt road and listen, watch the people dance in the pews, The Right Reverend Mother Blossom Gilford presiding.

We always came after services started so as not to disturb the congregation as they entered and we talked quietly among ourselves during the sermon so as not to be disrespectful or get chased away (we weren't interested and couldn't hear it from our vantage anyway). Occasionally, someone would step out of the church for a cigarette or some fresh air. Some nodded politely; most pretended not to see us.

I longed to go to the LBJBC, but no white people ever went and it was always a full house.

They sang of sin and redemption. I imagined them praying for spiritual guidance and recounting frightening Bible stories. (There are some real scary ones!) You can't always explain matters of the spirit, but something came across that dirt road and wrapped its arms around me. The other kids loved the music as much as I did. Kids that were Catholic and Protestant and Atheist, we all listened. We were the Second Line Congregation of the Lord Baby Jesus Baptist Church until they raised the building over the foundation and closed the doors.

The entire congregation of the Lord Baby Jesus Church went to each funeral held there. Friends, relatives, acquaintances— long lines of cars and crowds of people showed up. I don't know where all the people came from; there certainly weren't that many people in our town. There certainly wasn't anyone living or dead who knew that many people. The turnout was always startling and took over the country roads around our town.

"Sweet harmony." "Water risin'" "Hallelujah!"
It's a fine way to go out.

~

New Orleans funerals are open to the public.
They're a celebration of life. If there hasn't
been a death in a while, the people organize a
funeral anyway.
The dead are buried above ground so that
water can't get to them. Water can, however,
get to the living.

It always comes back to water.

~

*"universal"* *"Mike Stang"*

The only thing I learned in high school chemistry is this: water is an international solvent. In time it can wear away anything. (I've known people like this.)

Science changes so frequently; is this still true? I think so.

~

I've been saved from death several times—not only from drowning and a near fatal birth, but from potential car accidents, drug reactions, childhood diseases, falls, bullies, asthma attacks, food poisoning—you get the picture. In New York, Louis and I came out of a movie late one night and I ran across the street ahead of him. The light changed and he was stuck on the other side. I started wandering slowly down the deserted street and a man grabbed me and pulled me into a dark narrow alley between buildings. "Don't try to run," he said.

I became liquid; my arms waved languidly and my wrists slid out of his hands. I turned and ran home. If he'd said, "Don't scream," would I have screamed?

Once I was coming home from a party on the back of a motorcycle. The boy who was driving was drunk and we were going about 100 mph. I made a deal with God that if HE got me home safely, I'd be a good girl forever. Other people have done this and kept their promise.

I haven't entirely kept mine. I hope God's forgiven me for breaking it—and for using a masculine pronoun in connection with holiness and creation.

My soul hasn't been officially "saved" though many people have offered their services. I'm not entirely sure about what I would be saving it for.

This is a strange attitude for me as I'm a saver at heart. I keep leftover food, old letters and greeting cards, teapots, my

grade school poetry, and plastic bags to reuse. I keep new
clothing "for good." Often the best articles of clothing I buy
get worn only a few times before they deteriorate or go out of
style because I rarely go places good enough to wear them. This
is frustrating and shameful. I get this habit from my mother
and her mother. I gave Gram Little a chic housecoat for her
ninety-fifth birthday and she said she'd "save it for good." I find
this ridiculous and yet, would probably do the same thing.

~

I've met people who seem to have no soul at all, yet I feel the
soul of my mother and other ancestors hovering near me at
times. I have no control over this phenomenon.

I seem to have very little control over most things but I'm
pretty good at being liquid, at keeping to my own nature in the
face of what I find in my path. Pretty good…

~~

Louis' cousin's daughter, Dana, wears way too much eye make-
up and dark clothing for a nineteen year old. The clothing,
piercings, and tattoos don't bother me, but Dana doesn't have
the faintest idea about why she dresses like this. She calls herself
"Goth" because she's seen Ozzy Osbourne on TV and lives in a
similarly nice house (her parents'), in a wealthy suburb.

She and her friend Andy visit various graveyards for fun.
I taught her how to do rubbings and she's gotten some great
ones. They're attracted to cemeteries for different reasons than
I am but I can't really explain their reasoning. It has something
to do with "coolness," a concept I never got the hang of.

She told me this story: She and Andy were driving around

in Connecticut one weekend and happened upon an old cemetery. They roamed through it for a bit and were drawn to two matching stones with space around them. They decided the couple buried there had been husband and wife. The husband's stone was blank except for his name. The wife's stone said "wife," and "Doubt the man who swears devotion." The implication is obvious.

Andy excused himself to go pee in the woods. Dana leaned against the stone to take in the sights. It was verging on twilight.

She swears that she heard a whisper behind her. "Stay away," she thought it said. But there wasn't anyone around. She couldn't see Andy.

"My man!"

Dana was so frightened that she fell running to the car and dropped the keys. Andy found her sobbing in the mud. He located the keys, with much difficulty, and drove her home.

Dana looked the couples name up on the Internet and found that the husband had been murdered twenty years before the wife died, stabbed thirty-six times in the back room of the hardware store he worked in. She's sure the wife killed him for cheating on her. She believes the wife was jealous of her that day in the cemetery and that she was lucky to escape with her life.

This story made Dana a celebrity among her friends.

I'm impressed, maybe a bit jealous that the dead chose to speak to them. It'll be something to tell their grandchildren.

~

Teenagers in my town used to go to the local cemetery to "make out." Often there'd be eight or ten cars parked at the Laural Hill Cemetery. I was the one who instigated friends to drive through Laural Hill with the bright lights on, blowing the horn to scare them.

I never understood why they called it the "submarine races?"

~

My father had his name inscribed on the double tombstone he bought for my mother and himself when she died. It had his birthdate and a hyphen followed by a space for his death date. I begged him not to do this, but he did it anyway. It bothered me to see it, but I visited her grave very seldom as I lived far away. He visited often.

As hard as I tried to draw him into my life and the lives of my husband and children, he was marking time until he could be with my mother. His spirit left with hers though his body was still here.

~

After my mother died, the church widows began calling my dad. He was embarrassed and wouldn't talk to them. I told him that men and women could be friends these days, they could have a meal together, go to a movie, or take a walk without romantic entanglements. He wouldn't hear of it. As much as I'd like to think people today feel this way, I don't think the church ladies that were near his age and lived in Smiggle's Bottom were aware of this any more than my dad. But then, I don't pretend to know what lonely church ladies think.

After cousin Cora's sister died, her husband married within a year. After Aunt Pauline died, her husband married his high school sweetheart eight months later. Some people don't know how to be alone; they're desperate for companionship. This seems to be true of men who were married for a long time. They complain about their wives when they're alive, but can't seem to live without them. Women are much more resilient. When Uncle Meritt died, Aunt Min went on a tear. She went to Paris and Las Vegas and California, all within the first two years. She took up folk dancing, yoga, and bought herself a bicycle. She had a good time.

I think Uncle Meritt should be happy about this. She spent a lot of years taking care of him and he was a grouchy old bird.

~

Over the rooftops of Cairo you can see the pyramids half hidden in a smoggy mist. Louis and I took a room at the Mena House Hotel, an old residence at the foot of the Great Pyramid. It's hard to believe that anyone actually lived there, but they had at one time. We got there late in the evening. I didn't sleep at all the first night and slept very little thereafter. The power of Pyramids is awesome, even with the drapes drawn. I was aware of them all night while Louis slept.

Bedouin men guarded the road to the Pyramids. At night they sat by their small fire. In the early dawn, women brought food and coffee (in brass urns, not Starbucks).

How does one get the job of being guardian of the Pyramids?

I can't imagine that there's an interview or a test; it's likely handed down through generations (and what would a Bedouin father do if his child wanted to be... say, a stockbroker instead?). If not handed down, there must be strict qualifications. First of all, you have to be a Bedouin; it's always been the job of Bedouins. And, alas, it seems you must be a man. This requirement has changed in many other occupations over the years. I imagine a group of fierce women with rifles and camels as the designated guards of the pyramids. I can imagine myself laughing with them at the fire, drinking strong Arabian coffee. But life there isn't what it was in the Arabian Nights and it's certainly not what life was like in Brooklyn where I lived then—or Harlem, where I now live. The Bedouin requirement leaves me out anyway.

At dawn, I looked out the window on the opposite side of the room and saw the sun rise over Cairo. The city was nestled in a golden mist. We'd been expected to sleep in the crosshairs of two mysteries. I wondered what kind of people would have presumed to live in such a place.

That morning we went up to the Pyramids on camels that were named Mickey Mouse and Michael Jackson. The boys that led them wore jeans and sneakers; you don't pretend to be anything other than yourself in the presence of such enigmatic mysteries.

The Sphinx, which appears so monumental in pictures, is much smaller in person (not unlike a lot of famous actors, I hear). The Pyramids overwhelm it completely.

You're permitted to go into the Great Pyramid through a narrow slanted passage. I come from a lineage of miners so I'm not at all claustrophobic, but this passage unnerved me. There was barely room for the visitors who were coming out, to pass you on the way down. There were a handful of other tourists experiencing it in their own languages. Still, it was eerie.

As bad as the passage was, the bottom chamber was worse, small and airless. It was like being dead—but not in a peaceful way. The pharaoh's belongings, those buried with him, had been taken out; some writing and pictures remained on the walls. I'm a person who fears heights and normally feels comforted by small contained spaces, even if they are underground. I stepped into this chamber, looked about me once, and went (rapidly) back out.

A pyramid is a place of great portent and power, not a place I would choose to spend eternity. Give me a peaceful, somewhat unkempt cemetery with fanciful headstones and a few shade trees.

I can't imagine what sort of people would commission such monuments as the pyramids. The Egyptians we met were pleasant and had a sense of humor. OK, some may have been a bit conniving, but no more than you'd find at any tourist attraction and they seemed very much in tune with life.

Ancient Egyptian culture revolved around Death. There is no humor in a Pyramid; it's a dead serious structure.

~

The Cairo Museum is like a warehouse. Objects are stacked against walls and on top of each other. Many of them do not have descriptions.

For a small extra fee, you can enter the Mummy Room. The Mummy Room is a sealed room kept at a constant temperature in order to keep the mummies from deteriorating. It's not as eerie as the interior of the Pyramids, but it's not comfortable—and this isn't the effect of temperature. The mummies are under glass, unwrapped, exposed to the eyes of strangers. It's invasive and embarrassing to see.

Even Norman Bates dressed his mother in the movie Psycho. These bodies are thousands of years old. Their organs were removed and placed in jars, their flesh treated with herbs and oils to preserve them. They didn't protest this fate; they looked forward to it. But they didn't expect their bodies to be scrutinized by living people thousands of years later.

I wished I could've lingered to hear the stories they had to tell; I'm sure they held some back from the scientists who unwrapped and studied them, and placed them in that room.

~~

There's no record of my mother or either set of grandparents on the internet. I could find no record of my Manx grandparents' immigration at Ellis Island, though I know there must be one. I have my grandmother and father's passport when they went back for a year; my father was six years old.

If you Google me, you get information about things I've written and done. Some of this information is embarrassing though I'm not embarrassed of the one piece of porno I published.

An obituary of my father appears on a website with obituaries of other magicians. As a result of seeing this, a distant relative of my grandfather (my father's father) contacted me. He sent me a photo of my grandfather with eight of his fourteen siblings. With it was a genealogy that went back to the 1600s. Most of the men listed had been miners. Some had come to America and settled in places like Colorado and California in the mid 19th century, the Gold Rush Era. My father hadn't known any of this. The miners all died young—you'd think they'd learn a lesson from the experiences of their forefathers and take up different occupations.

My father went into the mines only once, when he was a child. My grandfather told him "You do NOT want to do this."

Sometimes it takes generations to accept the fact that things can't go on as they have if we are to survive.

~

Louis does not appear on the internet but he has relatives with elaborate websites. My children will have extensive internet presence. Perhaps thousands of years from now, strangers in pajamas will be looking at us from their homes. What will they learn from our mistakes?

~

TRADITIONAL TIBETANS HAVE THREE TYPES OF BURIAL: AN EARTH BURIAL, A WATER BURIAL, AND A SKY BURIAL. IN THE SKY BURIAL, YOU'RE CUT UP INTO LITTLE PIECES AND THROWN OFF THE TOP OF A MOUNTAIN. IF I WAS A TIBETAN IN ANOTHER LIFE, I DON'T REMEMBER WHAT KIND OF BURIAL I HAD.

~

The women who stoop over short brooms to sweep the courtyard aren't permitted to speak to the monks. Most of them are afraid to look up when the monks pass through. They're fearful of gazing upon holiness with earthly eyes. They stare down at their own rough hands and the dust that's accumulated in the courtyard.

The monks look down as they pass; they see only the thick ankles and worn shoes of women who work in the courtyard. They see only frayed hems and the dusty straw of the brooms.

If only one or the other would look up, they might find devotion.

~~

The cemetery where Louis' family's buried is just off a major highway that goes through a suburb of New York City. Cars whiz by at high speeds unless they're visiting the cemetery, then they slow down to the required fifteen miles an hour or less. There are few trees and bushes. The land is flat. The stones are mostly ordinary and none are older than 1970. A few large markers are obscenely modern. It's the strip-mall of cemeteries. People leave flowers at the graves and small pebbles on the markers. Still, there's a starkness about the place. It's as if the people were exiled from life.

The cemetery where my parents, my Manx grandfather, and Uncle Ernest are buried is hilly and green. The tombstones go back to the middle 1800s; many of them have epitaphs. They're simple in a gothic kind of way. Beside flowers, on holidays the graves are decorated appropriately—flags, Easter crosses, Halloween pumpkins, Christmas ornaments. Some people decorate their family gravesites with photos and objects they might have used in their lives. One woman has wooden spoons and an old cooking pot filled with flowers. Some children have teddy bears or dolls. One man has two cans of Iron City beer.

The groundskeeper has a tiny cottage on a hill right in the middle, the better to watch over his flock.

There are benches strategically placed for the mourners' comfort.

One of my favorite places in the world is Greenwood Cemetery in Brooklyn. It dates from 1838 and is 478 acres of spectacular landscape, statuary and mausoleums. Its "residents" are the famous and infamous. It even has live parrots nesting in the entry arches. There are tours and events, history and a tasteful Halloween display.

It's quiet and beautiful, a grand place to spend a day or an eternity.

# Chapter 16

## "Onlys" and Firsts

Near the plots where my family is buried, is the grave of Alice Flood. Mrs. Flood was a Manx woman and friend of my grandmother. She owned six small cottages on a lake in West Virginia. Every summer, my parents and I vacationed at Mrs. Flood's cottages on Window Lake. While my parents slept-in in the mornings, I had tea and toast with Mrs. Flood. Mr. Flood was long dead by the time I came around.

Mrs. Flood was a pleasant lumpy sort of woman who lived in a small cottage by herself. Her house was cluttered with porcelain objects, shells, and African Violets. Each object had a story and each African Violet had to be nurtured carefully. African Violets are notoriously fragile. Both of my grandmothers kept them. I wouldn't dare.

Mrs. Flood and I enjoyed each other immensely and talked long into the morning. Conversations between convivial old women and young children are sacred and frivolous. (I'm fortunate to have such conversations with my own grandchildren.) My father would collect me when they were ready to go to the lake. M loved the sun, but Pop's red hair and sensitive skin kept him in the shade. He did love the water though, and was always the one to go in with me while M watched from the shore.

Some days, Pop and I would rent a bicycle-built-for-two and ride around the town and countryside together. In the evenings the three of us would go into town for supper and browse in the souvenir shops. I bought a white Navy hat there that I wore for years.

My favorite place was the "arcade." It wasn't an arcade in the modern sense of the word. There were no video games back then. It had skeet ball games, fortune-telling and strength-revealing machines, some pinball machines and a device that engraved your name or initials on a coin. The best, and most frustrating, was the claw machine. We never got one good thing from the claw machine. Aim for a bracelet and you got a can opener; aim for a Voodoo doll and you got an ugly little stuffed dog.

I had my first "date" the summer I was twelve at Mrs. Flood's. I don't remember the boy's name, but we had some races in the water and he kept bothering me after. I sat on my towel, too shy to talk while he and my mother yakked away. I hoped she would shut up and he would go away, but that didn't happen. She told him my name and all about me, and she asked questions about him. They had a fine time embarrassing me.

"Do you think Felicity could come to the arcade with me this evening after supper?" he asked. I shock my head "No," but this was apparently unacceptable.

"Oh, come on honey. It sounds like fun," she said. "You love the arcade. Of course she'll go."

I could have killed her.

Worse than that, she treated it like a real date. "What are you going to wear?" "We should clean your sneakers."—that kind of talk. It made me VERY nervous. I don't remember what I wore, but I'm sure I wore my Navy hat pulled down over my eyes and Keds as I did in all the photos of those summers.

He actually had the nerve to have two coins engraved with our names and the date on them, one for me, one for him. But he bought me ice cream so I let him get away with it.

The "date" wasn't as unpleasant as sitting with him and M at the lake and I dreaded the next day. But he must have gone home because I don't remember a second date or another uncomfortable threesome at the lake. He might have kissed me goodnight; I don't remember.

In fact, I can't say that I remember my first kiss at all. It must have been terribly uneventful. My mother remembered hers. She remembered her first kiss, her first date, her first dance, her first pair of high heels. I'm sure she remembers all her "firsts" but we didn't go any further.

~

I would never ask my father about his "firsts." He was a shy private man. His memory wasn't very good for that kind of thing anyway. He remembered everything that had to do with his job and every magician and magic trick he'd ever seen. When he did shows, he said the same exact thing every time; he called it his "patter."

~

My memory's never been good and is getting worse in my dotage. This usually shocks older people but when you've had the problem all your life, it doesn't much bother you. Often what I remember are the spaces between—blank walls, uncomfortable silences punctuating conversations, once empty lots that have sprouted tall buildings, meaningless looks. When I can't remember, I make it up, which means that I pretty much make up my life as I go along.

Having a bad memory doesn't necessarily mean you're stupid, but I admit that I wasn't great at school. I did a lot of daydreaming. I should've failed algebra, but Mr. Lieb had the compassion to give me a passing grade. What's the point of algebra anyway? I've gotten along nicely without it. I was the wiz kid in Geometry though. I never missed a problem and the teacher used to bring especially hard problems for me to do at the board while he taught the other kids. I was able to do every one he gave me. I never missed a problem, 100%! It's an easy subject; all you have to do is learn a few rules at the beginning of the year and spend the rest of the time applying them. I can "apply" as well as anyone.

Now, if I could only remember the rules...

~

The Tale Of the Glass Man

There was once a man who was made of glass. He was usually very careful to keep his stomach covered for when it was bared, people were hypnotized by its intricate workings, the multihued liquids that churned in its depths, the minute organisms that dwelled in its folds, the kaleidoscopic dance of biomechanical operations. Crowds formed, traffic stopped, mothers dropped the hands of their children, lovers lost each other, and emergencies were forgotten.

The man of glass shed shards when he saw how easily the fleshy ones were distracted from their own lives to look at him. He was surprised that they were not interested in the exposed ankles of their women or the silky hair that blew in the wind. He was distraught that no one considered his feelings or asked about his thoughts, assuming that these were transparent too. They stared at the pulsations of his heart and, in public bathrooms, snickered at the plumbing in his genitals.

The man of glass would never have bared his stomach had he

not been offended by their flippant attitude. "Oh, him," they said. "We can see through him." It was as if he wasn't there. "Really," he'd say. "Well, see through this." He was always sorry after he'd lifted his shirt and everything around him stopped. He wished there was a way to see through the fleshy ones, but he never found one.

It was a lonely life for the man of glass and cracks began to appear. The grinding in his feet curtailed his mobility. An increasing number of chips caused his clothing to tear and snag. He could no longer wear sweaters and the cold winters caused him to crack more. Still, he kept himself clean with Windex. Even when a woman drove into him with her car and he was shattered, he continued to go about his daily routine in pieces. Then one day, in the course of building a superhighway, a powerful wrecking machine swept its steel arm at him. With one stroke, he was gone. Tiny pieces of him shone in the sunlight for a while and then were ground into the earth.

Some tales have no moral; they're just stories. What can we learn from a man of glass? None of us are made of such material...

Then again, sometimes others know us better than we know ourselves.

~

My father convinced me that my feet were ugly. He didn't do this out of malice; it was something he truly believed. "Of all the things you could have inherited from me, you ended up with my feet," he'd say. "What a shame."

I spent a lot of years being self-conscious about my feet. The truth is that they aren't ugly at all and neither were my father's.

In fact, my feet are rather attractive. I have no bunions, unsightly calluses, corns or strange bumps, no hammer toes. I have a perfectly good arch and strong ankles. My feet have taken me a long way.

There was nothing wrong with my father's feet either; it was his ears he should have worried about. His ears were enormous! Had his feet been ugly, they would have been hidden by socks and shoes anyway, but you can't hide ears. He wore his hair short even through the sixties and seventies. He was a very proper gentleman, not given to popular trends. How was it that he never noticed his ears?

"Big" doesn't necessarily mean "ugly." My father's large ears were rather spectacular. They weren't distorted in any way other than size. They were the size of a child's hand. Even though his head was large, his ears were still disproportionate.

One would think that his hearing might match the generous proportion of these organs. Not so. Though he claimed that his hearing was normal, he often heard what he wanted rather than what was being said.

Have I inherited this trait? Or do I hear what's being said and don't always understand it?

Listen to this:

I imagine my Manx grandfather's ghost lingering to watch his boys grow up. Perhaps he is just a reflection in a window of an old house, a man sitting in a Mission style chair, behind him a dark, sparse room. The people in the house might not notice him; they're so busy going about their lives. He's a small man with coal dust embedded in the lines of his face, barely visible in the shadowy room. He's a man who worked very hard; you can tell by his hands, gnarled and muscular. He sits near an old stove to keep warm and watches out of the window across the room. When his family isn't at home, he can hear mice running in the hollow walls, sounds of life.

He watches the men go into the mines and watches them come out. If he was alive he'd be breathing in darkness and coal

154

dust like them. He watches faded women in house-dresses go about their work in raw light. He watches children who are not carefree; they go into the mines at a young age. He keeps his vigil day and night, day and night.

He remembers a time when he was alive, though barely, sitting at the same window. His old friend, Philip Grace, came every few days to share a sandwich and bring him cigarettes. He told Philip he was doing fine, and Philip never asked what he saw from the window. Once a day grandmother would bring him warm water to bathe in and clean clothes. She helped him dress. Miss Elulalie came to check his temperature and blood pressure, listen to his breathing. There were too many sick miners for the company doctor to visit often and Elulalie was a competent nurse. "*That was a particularly fine hat you wore to church on Sunday,*" he'd tell her. She'd be embarrassed, but pleased that someone noticed.

He won't remember his painful death, but will find himself at his window afterward. Perhaps the ghosts of Philip Grace and Miss Elulalie will attend him again after a while.

His ghost would be waiting the day the mine shut down. Only a few families would remain in the town, those with nowhere else to go. He'd see the Union officials slip away in big cars, their wallets stuffed with (un)dues. He'd watch people pick up their Relief checks in embarrassment and try to scratch vegetable gardens into the hard contaminated earth. From his window he couldn't see the abandoned shafts collapse, but he could watch houses sink into the earth and smell the gasses that rose up from abandoned mines. He could watch weeds grow on slag heaps; men sleep in abandoned coke ovens. He would notice that after a while trains rarely passed by, then not at all. He could smell the cheap whiskey as it was passed hand to hand.

This would be difficult for even a ghost to watch; the mice in the wall would become maddening. Landscape and people would become distorted as he faded away, edges of past times dissolved.

Would there have been even a faint trace of him to greet me when I arrived?

~

Ghosts are less substantial than shadows. Shadows are the proof of reality. There's a moment each day when there are no natural shadows. The only shadows are those contrived by unnatural light. You must hold very still until the shadows stir again and the world spins. Many people are unaware of this and persist in what they're doing. This is why some pursuits become futile or are corrupted.

The masked man watches for shadows in order to catch the villain. The rogue commits lies in the light and we look away.

~

We take on the traits of our dead ancestors and perhaps some of their energy. Do they see out of our eyes? Do they return to guide us?

How were Louis and I related in another life? In many other lives? When we first met I used to pick his dirty shirts up off the floor, smell the familiar scent and try to remember. Now I lay my head on the warm spot in the bed after he gets up—this is especially comforting in the afternoons after his nap.

There are photos of us as bride and groom gleeful and carefree. Only one was taken much later when we were exhausted. In other pictures, Louis looks like a happy magician in a top hat. I look like a nun with flowers. I'm cuter than I remember. That picture hung in our bathroom for many years. I try to imagine us with our feet buried in cake or in funny clothes from another time

~

I've never been the center of attention except in the presence of my parents and that was always uncomfortable. I'm content being at the periphery. OK, I've had the "rock star dream" like everyone else but I'm more likely to be happy when I can watch unnoticed. Often I don't understand the requirements well enough to participate. I admire, but don't envy others who do. I share in their joy and pride, turn away at their embarrassment, and stand beside them in sadness.

I listen when they speak, even though they may not think I do, (OK, maybe not always) but I've no answers to offer them. They inspire me; they horrify me; they amuse me; they anger me. I find companions everywhere.

Reality doesn't always make sense; it isn't always valid. The world isn't flat but rounded, sound and experiences are spiral.

~

Rosemary didn't know who her mother was. She was thankful for her adoptive parents and she gathered people around her throughout her life. She never married and didn't care to find her birth parents. She hoped they'd feel the same about her.

When her adoptive parents died, she gathered more people about her; she made her own family from those she met. As a nurse she accumulated lonely sick people. As a neighbor and tennis player, she accumulated others.

What do you call a relative you have chosen or have been chosen by? This is a very special relationship. Rosemary chose people she had affection for, but her adoptive parents chose her as a baby, before they could have had any affection for her. Their affection grew, as hers for them.

Many of us are related to people by accident. Other cultures have words for these relationships. They have different obligations attached to them. Our customs are much more primitive. Sometimes those related to us by affection are closer than those related by blood. Here's a poem about such a person...

## Back In West Virginia We Play Pool At the Met With Abby, Her New Husband And an Old Absence

Abby's grandfather owned a general store where
my grandmother worked as milliner stitching
flowers and feathers and veiling. But
we didn't know that for a long time...

Before Ethan,
Abby and I were in a jug band and
shared rooms on Jones St. and
waitress summers on the Cape. Everyone
loved Ethan,
hippies and frat boys, professors
and janitors. But  Abby
loved him best.

Then
it was me and Louis and Abby and Ethan,
pinball and pickled eggs at Oggies,
IC Rockers and road trips.
Hey, Bo Diddley.
Until...Louis and I
U-Hauled out of West Virginia into
the world.

The saddest night was when Patty called
to say Ethan was wrapped around a tree
in Volkswagen and oblivion. Abby
took butter out of the fridge and
spread grief
on burnt toast and biscuits. Little Danny, and Charlotte
and Lisie (who was named after me, sort of)

went to stay with her sister—
we were far away and bound
by another life. But car and tree and memory
wrapped around us (some
tighter than others).

Grandparents and store, swathed
in timeless speculation and coal dust
while death came on black ice, flowered,
                    feathered
                    and veiled.

# Chapter 17

## Split Peas

Sometimes you can tell when someone's ready to die. The sky turns ominous and the small hairs on the back of your neck prickle. This happened when my mother died, but I didn't pay attention.

Sometimes death is a complete surprise.

Toddlers fall off of boats and drown; great uncles get hit by cars. Soldiers get blown up or shot. Aging teachers with lymphoma that they never told you about, fade away and don't recognize you when you visit them at the hospital. You sit there for hours anyway, so that the family might have a meal or go home and shower. Friends have babies that are born dead and their husband asks you to go to the house and remove all the baby things before they get home from the hospital. I'm not sure this is a comfort for them when they return.

~~

I don't like to see plastic flowers at cemeteries. I prefer the tradition of immortelles, decorative objects made of beads and wire that were placed on graves in the past. This was common in France and England in the late 1800s and early 1900s and some places in America. Often they were made into wreaths. In some cases odd trinkets, hair, photos, other memorabilia were woven into them. It's a lovely idea.

I'm generally in favor of offerings and notes placed in

coffins. The Chinese, ever practical and frugal, burn paper representations of money and objects for the use of their loved ones in the next world. Historically, they're the most reverential toward their ancestors. They're the ones that came up with the concept of "hungry ghosts." What would they say about my mother?

~

Folks in Northern Appalachia tell a lot of tales, old and new, fact and fancy. But my old neighbor Dirt Yankovic swears the story of Alby Kooser is truth and Dirt may not be what you'd call a solid citizen, but he's not given to making up stories unless it's to get himself out of some predicament.

The story goes like this: First Alby's grandmother died. Granny Kooser was 103 and lived in a "home" in Ohio. Dirt hadn't seen her for a good ten years. Alby's mother called to tell him that, in the midst of a heated bingo game, Granny heaved a great sigh, closed her eyes and stopped breathing.

"You seen her fer yourself?" he asked. Like Gram Little, the old lady had gone on for so long, it seemed impossible that she was dead.

That night when Alby took off his sock, he noticed that the two smallest toes on his left foot were missing. He turned his sock inside out and two shriveled greenish objects fell on the bed. They looked like peas. Alby put them in a jar and put the jar on top of the refrigerator. He forgot about them and ate his supper of chipped ham and IC Lite.

He decided that there was no reason for him to leave his marijuana crop to West Virginia rabbits at a crucial stage in the growth cycle, so he didn't drive up to Ohio for the funeral. However, he couldn't stop thinking about Gram's apple crumble, and at supper his lower lip suddenly splashed into his glass of ginger beer. Alby fished it out with two fingers and dropped it like hot buckshot when he realized what it was. Slowly, it shriveled up and took on a greenish tinge. Alby added the "pea" to the jar and studied himself in the mirror. His lower lip had protruded unnaturally, he'd looked as if he was always pouting. He decided he looked better without it. His upper lip was sufficiently plump to cover his teeth and he liked the strong look of his chin without the lower hanging over it. He saw no need to panic.

Alby pulled his old army jacket over his scrawny body, called his dog Digger into the back of the Ford pick-up, and headed down Three Mile Hill to Wanda's Beer City. Roselma Spear was hunkered up to the bar, her limp hair like a wad of used cotton, yellowed and forgotten, but her breasts pointed right at him when she turned to say, "Hey, Alby."

Alby sucked down enough Rolling Rocks with Roselma to forget he'd left Digger in the back of the pick-up. Sometime after midnight they heard the sound of squealing breaks and a dull thud. Digger lay by the side of the road stiff and bleeding. Alby put him in the truck, took him home, and buried him in his favorite spot under the porch.

The next morning Alby was missing his left hand and there were six more peas in the jar. He thought of going to see Doc Shoebecki, but a frost set in and he had to pick his "crop"—with one hand. He felt no physical pain.

Three nights later Roselma stopped by and Alby, who didn't want her to know about his diminishing condition, insulted her from behind the screen door so she wouldn't come in. She was so angry, she stormed off screaming, "I never want to see you again Alby Kooser."

That night his left foot fell off and Alby watched it shrivel up. It took three hours for it to achieve its final pea size. He hobbled out to the yard and found a thick branch to walk with. What would he tell people? What could he tell Doc Shoebecki?

Alby decided to check his liquor supply before he headed down to see the doctor. He found a gallon of Boone's Farm and a bottle and a half of cheap tequila. It took him two days to finish it all and by that time the "crop" had begun to dry and he set into packing it up.

A week later, and a few more gallons of Boone's Farm, Alby's mother's heart gave out—his father being long gone—and Alby's right ear ended up in the jar with the other "peas."

Alby sobered up real fast. He sold off what was left of this crop to Dirt Yankovic who told him, "You don't look so good, buddy."

"Just take the shit and git outta here," Alby growled.

"You sure you don't need some help?"

"What I need, ain't no one left can give it to me. Now git!"

After that, Alby sat at the kitchen table staring at the contents of the jar, or on the porch watching the world recede behind Three Mile Hill. Each evening he watched the sun set, and felt his mother and Granny and Digger sink further into the past with it. Each evening another part of him would fall off and Alby would place the "pea" in the jar with the others. He wrote Dirt a note explaining what was happening and apologizing for his behavior, but he never got out to mail it.

When Dirt finally came to check on him, he found the note

wadded up on the floor. The jar was less than half-full and a few peas lay scattered on the table and high-backed chair. "Outside," he said, "birds fluttered around the trees, crickets screeched and a few wild dogs circled the cabin looking for scraps. Everything seemed normal." But Alby Kooser was never seen again.

~

When my mother died, we looked for a diamond pin that had belonged to my Manx grandmother. It was the only good piece of jewelry in the family. Nigel Skifflington must have given it to her. We couldn't find it anywhere, though my father and I were too distraught to look very well. My mother must have hidden it as a precaution against robbers. It was an unfortunate loss but as you know, the pin may be gone but my mother is not entirely lost.

Mostly you accumulate "stuff" when someone dies. You take all those meaningful things and put them in your house or relatives send you boxes of "stuff" from an aunt or a cousin's house. When your house is crammed with these things, you try to give them away but no one else is emotionally attached to them so you end up donating them. It's difficult to make the decision to get rid of these things, but once it's gone, it's a relief, so do it.

~

Until the seventeenth century, most people were wrapped in shrouds and buried in the earth or in tombs (Tibetans, Mayans, some others were exceptions). Time and materials were too valuable to be wasted. It wasn't until the mid or late seventeen hundreds that coffins became status symbols. Poor people got pine boxes; rich people got exotic woods, stained and polished handles, locks, nameplates and other ornaments. Metals came into use in the 1800s, along with lining, padding, and windows. Since then, all kinds of metals have been used; I read that they tried making a coffin out of India rubber once.

When my mother died, my father and I had to choose a coffin. It was the first coffin I'd ever chosen. We were taken into a room full of metal boxes that looked like horizontal refrigerators; there was a choice of colors.

I buried both parents in wooden coffins.

~

My memory is so unreliable that I often wonder if my past really happened. Much of it seems strange and absurd. Most people I talk to believe their past is quite realistic even though it might sound strange and absurd to me. I trust they're correct about this as they remember most other things much better than I do. Louis can find his way to anywhere he's ever been; he remembers the history of almost every rock 'n roll group and sports figure. But he loses his glasses at least once a week and we don't bother to give him house keys any more because he's lost so many.

My mother used to say that she didn't believe in reincarnation because if there had been other lives my son, Harlie, would surely remember as he never forgot anything. Harlie did remember a lot of stuff until he hit puberty, then he couldn't remember things like closing the door of the refrigerator, or where he left his history book.

Some people remember every book they've read, every film the've seen. I can't tell you how many times I bought a book twice, thinking I hadn't read it, and I routinely rent movies I've seen before. Sometimes I don't realize it until I'm halfway (or more) through.

I don't remember names unless they're really strange. Bligh and Vroom, I remember, but forget Bob and Amy.

What's true for me is not always "real." Have I said that before?

~

Sometimes there are long intervals in our lives when we live day to day and nothing extraordinary happens. The vacuum breaks down, the kids fight, dinner's ruined, you watch TV even though there's nothing on. Your favorite bands don't tour and movies are all car chases, explosions, and bad dialogue. Kids are your biggest excitement and *James and the Giant Peach* is the best book you've read in years.

Life is not always poetic.

The eighties might have rocked for some people, but not for me. They were just a lot of jarring music, bad hair and bad clothes. I didn't participate.

You'd think I would have slept more out of the boredom of the eighties. I didn't. This is when I started calling my "sleep problem" insomnia. If sleep is the closest we get to death, what does it mean that mine is so disturbed.

I don't sleep more than three hours at a clip. I get up, read a while, drink some relaxing tea, take a pill sometimes… even if I'm exhausted; in fact, the more exhausted I am, the less I sleep. I blame this on my children who never routinely slept through the night until they hit puberty—then they slept all the time. But this is not entirely fair; I was never a good sleeper. My mother told me that I was a "head banger" when I was a baby.

As a child I remember lying in bed, rocking back and forth, and singing for hours before I fell asleep. This never seemed to bother my parents even though we lived in places with very thin walls. Perhaps head-banging and insomnia are the reasons my memory is so tenuous and random.

Until I had children, I had problems falling asleep. Now I fall asleep relatively easily but can't stay asleep. Often I'm in bed for nine hours in order to get five hours of sleep. I'm an expert on sunrises as I'm usually up before the sun. I've seen it pop up over mountain tops, ooze out from behind trees, conceal itself in golden hazes, and hide behind dark clouds refusing to surrender 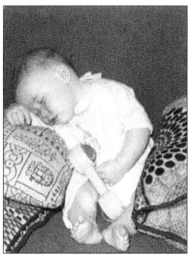 even a scrap of light. Some mornings it dyes the world blood red, and some mornings it saps all the color out of the vista and leaves us in black and white like an old movie. Usually some light leaks out before the actual sunrise. In the country, this wakes animals: roosters crow, coyotes howl, dogs make preliminary rounds to check their territory before going back to sleep. Cities that rarely stop for anything become calm in the early morning. The guard changes, night-people make their way home, day-people begin to emerge. Neither are fully awake.

I always liked mornings. I have the world to myself. I do a series of slow exercises, Qi Gong and Tai Chi (sometimes with swords). Afterward, on cold mornings, I cuddle up to Louis, who's like a hairy fireplace.

The hours I'm awake in the middle of the night are more difficult. Thoughts ricochet, anxiety arises even when there's no reason for it. Often in the country, the loud sound-wall of insects suddenly stops, abandoning the world to deafening silence. I imagine wild animals, monsters, murderers, lunatics outside. Trees blow, the sky revolves; I feel isolated. I become uneasy, afraid that something dire is afoot and I'm destined to be its victim. Too much quiet is suspicious.

This is when it's good to have a dog around. Dogs know if there's really something wrong. Their sleep is not disturbed by misread sound or lack of it.

~

The white noise of city never stops. It lulls me into a (false?) sense of security. Someone's always there, watching out. I turn on my reading light. Outside the window, other lights glitter. My light is small. I know somewhere on the other side of the world it's day and people are eating, dancing, making love, mourning their dead.

When I was a child, living in the Fourgoose house, the pear tree made shadow plays on my wall. One windy night, shadow monsters put a curse on me and sent frogs, hundreds of them, to cavort on my bedroom floor. I was afraid to get out of bed. I didn't know what the frogs would do to me; I didn't want to step on them, feel their slime. My dad heard my calls for help and broke the curse by coming in.

There's only been one curse put on me since then that I know of, and that didn't work. After our children left for college, we rented a cottage we owned in the country to an Indonesian woman. She was a problem from day one, the tenant from Hell. She was noisy and unclean: her children broke things and she complained about all sorts of nonexistent problems. We kept her deposit to make repairs when she left, and she sued us for it. We had photographs of the house before she came and after she moved out, so of course, we won. In frustration, she wrote a letter invoking bad Karma on us forever. She didn't scare us because we'd done nothing wrong; she was the culprit. Our Karma's been fine, but that was the end of our landlord days. We sold the cottage. Good riddance!

NEVER BE AFRAID OF SOMEONE CURSING YOU IF YOU'RE IN THE RIGHT. CURSES ON THE INNOCENT ARE UNJUST AND PEOPLE WHO MAKE THEM OUT OF VENGEANCE OR MALICE ARE RARELY SUCCESSFUL. (BUT KEEP YOUR SECRET NAME JUST IN CASE.)

~

An exception to this rule was my cousin Earl, Aunt Kat's son. Had Earl lived in a tribal culture, a shaman would have been called to exorcize the demons from him. He rattled and shook, repeated his demands endlessly until they were met. "Momma, I want an egg. Please make me an egg. I wanna egg! Where's my egg? Why won't you make me an egg? Egg! Egg! Please give me eggs!" This would go on until he got his eggs or Aunt Kat beaned him with the pan. If it was something that couldn't be provided, it might go on for hours. He was the poster child for Prozac or whatever they give obsessive/compulsives these days, only he was born thirty years too early.

Earl was terrible at school but luckily, he inherited the Little Family idiot-savant condition. He was a wiz at fixing small mechanical devices. He couldn't hold a job, but people for miles around brought him their mixers and lawn mowers.

Earl's policy was make a dollar, spend a dollar. He spent his money on mechanical gizmos and collected painted rocks. Earl never learned to tie his shoes.

~

Didn't we all, at one time, fear stepping on a crack in the sidewalk? Did we make sure our food was separate when we were children, that the peas didn't get into the mashed potatoes? In my father's desk drawers, all the pencils were lined up, erasers facing one way, points the other, paperclips in their box, papers neatly stacked.

My mother made a distinction between dish towels and tea towels in the kitchen. Do you dry your hands with dish or teas? I never could remember.

I save all my buttons in jelly jars. No piece of clothing is thrown out with its buttons intact. Each jar holds a different color of button. When a button's lost, there's rarely a match in one in any of my jars. When I was little and my mother sewed, she would give me a tin full of buttons and I strung them on thread. This was a common occupation for children of my generation who had mothers that sewed. It worked to keep me busy but it's not as beneficial for hand-eye coordination as Xbox.

Pots and pans make excellent toys for children, possibly the best all-around playthings in the world. They can be played as musical instruments, worn, filled with water and emptied, stacked like blocks, sat in, packed with toys, spun like tops, used as weapons—the possibilities are limitless.

Children also love boxes.

I didn't inherit any of the Little family idiot-savant traits. Except for geometry, I'm not exceptionally good at anything.

My one talent used to be spitting. I was a champ when I was a kid and I'm still pretty good at it. I think allergies are the key to good spitting. You need volume and a certain amount of weight. When you have allergies there's always mucus available to mix with your saliva. Another key is to look innocent. No one expects a "nice girl" to spit well. Look demure, make a quick spit, then look about naively and no one will suspect it was you who did the spitting, or they'll be so shocked they won't be able to react.

Spitting is a reason you should always be nice to your waitresses.

# Chapter 18

## Everyone has Cancer

Uncle is dying. He wasn't a good man in his lifetime, which is why he has no one to care for him. His wife has stayed on grudgingly, but she relies heavily on me. Unfortunately, the phones don't work and the repairman is having chemo. I can't leave my home during the day because of workmen removing asbestos from the basement and radioactive waste from under the ground.

So I visit uncle at night while his wife gets a few hours rest. I've done this for several weeks now and before that, I drove him to his treatments. My car is badly in need of an oil change, but the mechanics are having their melanomas incised.

Uncle's very weak now, excruciatingly thin with huge tumors distending his head, limbs and body. He's acquired the appearance of ET, a bad man turned pathetically cute by an insidious disease. His voice has become childlike and he murmurs innocent fantasies. I never enjoyed Uncle's company, until now. The disease has rendered him harmless and amusing. It's the same disease, in a slightly different form, that affects the servicemen and mechanics.

To make matters worse, my computer's contracted a similar affliction. The instruction booklets call it a "virus," but I find it much more serious. In my unwittingly extensive oncologic experience, I've known similar malignant transformations. Early symptoms often go unrecognized or minimized, but I'm fated to foresee cancer in a random assortment of warning sings. I mentioned this to my genetic counsellor who referred me to a cooperative human tissue retrieval network. They've yet to return my call.

Uncle's wife, the dispassionate Margarita, is experiencing symptoms of fatigue, weight loss, pain and a marked change in bowel habits. She attributes this to the stress caused by attending to a dying man who she no longer loves. The long-suffering, and oddly behaved, Margarita had one foot out the door when Uncle was diagnosed. She consented to remain with him under the stipulation that she be permitted to pursue her own personal and career goals. For this reason, I agreed to accompany Uncle to his treatments. She pursues her opportunities between episodes of treatment-related complications. She addresses these problems basically by calling upon me at odd hours. We both persevere.

I've suggested that she contact her physician regarding blood-work for herself, biopsy, x-ray, mammogram, CT scan and Barium enema. She admitted to me that she no longer has a doctor as hers retired due to an early diagnosis of lymphoma. I haven't told her that I've detected the presence of hydrocarbons and alkylating agents in their home as she wouldn't believe that I'm acutely sensitive to such substances.

I'm not shocked that the check-out girl at the Gunn County Farmers Market has undergone a radical mastectomy. I am shocked to hear that the produce man, whose recommendations I've heeded unconditionally for 20 years, has a prostate the size of a honey melon. I'm hoping this condition has more to do with predisposition and inherited factors than exposure to provisions of which I partake as well.

Other members of the family have begun to gather in anticipation of Uncle's imminent demise. They discuss their own experiences with colon, kidney, and bladder, while smoking Marlboros. They don't stay long, but return to the Home Away Motel to sit by the pool and soak up ultraviolet radiation.

I attempt to read a thesis on new protocols while Uncle sleeps, but it doesn't hold my attention as much as the medical dramas on TV. Unfortunately, many of the original actors have been replaced, in order for them to undergo surgery or radiation treatments. The woman who plays the senior nurse on my favorite drama had a double mastectomy recently. She was written out of many episodes, but she's back sporadically now, albeit thinner and somewhat lethargic. She often holds a clipboard or medical apparatus in front of her chest. Alas, it seems unrealistic that I'll be able to read a significant number of the 1700 clinical trial abstracts that I have at my disposal.

The more distant relatives, who've come to see Uncle, tell Margarita what a brave man he is, uncomplaining and cheerful. She and I know that it's the combination of drugs he's given daily, thalidomide and morphine, steroids, mood enhancers, and vitamin cocktails that make him tolerant of his condition. Conversely, it's the tenacious Margarita, drugless, who accommodates a man she doesn't like, his distrustful niece, and various intrusive and discomforting relatives. It's the resolute Margarita who keeps the children recklessly cheerful and entertains us with droll banter and individually wrapped sweets. Perhaps, had she married someone else, she would be less cynical. Then again, what does a life of indulgence prepare you for? For the soon-to-be-liberated Margarita certainly led a pampered life before meeting Uncle. It was her great disappointment that he broke his promise to indulge her further (her expectations are remarkable indeed!)

I have to interrupt my vigil to attend the memorial of a college friend, a somewhat well-known artist who will be hailed as a genius now that she's dead. She may have succumbed to the toxic chemicals she used in her art. At her memorial, many people speak. Each person remembered something different

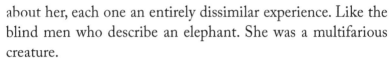

about her, each one an entirely dissimilar experience. Like the blind men who describe an elephant. She was a multifarious creature.

Electric wires crackle above Uncle's little house and gas escapes from the abandoned mines below, but we remain jovial and compassionate toward those less fortunate: for instance Mrs. Collymore on the street below, whose young daughter is now undergoing bone marrow aspiration for a condition complicated by pericardial disease; Byron Moldin, who is now experiencing thrombocytopenia as a result of his therapy; and the Hubert family in which eight of thirteen family members have some form of Hodgkin's or non-Hodgkin's lymphoma.

"It would be nice to lose twenty pounds before the Fall fashions hit the mall," Margarita comments wistfully.

I prefer to attribute this attitude to mania caused by a dire situation.

I often dream of primordial meadows and pristine waters as a backdrop for benign creatures, undefiled by interferon or toxicity. But alas I awake to pestilence and pathology, fever, hemorrhage, nausea, seizure, tumors, neuropathy, trauma and collapse (albeit, not all at once or manifest in a single individual). Even the trees outside Uncle's window have acquired lesions; the grass and foliage carry the stigma of contamination. It saddens me that in the embodiment of splendor, we must assume the presence of invisible microbes, smoldering bacteria and virus, ambushing pathogens.

As I listen to Uncle's tortured breathing, the defiant Margarita dons the blue silk dress that is her protective attire and begins a psychoactive dialogue reinforced by palliative movements, her effort to disinfect the whorl of extinction. The relatives are mortified but I'm envious of her ability to revel in disregard. I'm too innocent, awe-struck, and pathetic to participate. She shouts the news of the day to Uncle who blinks his bewilderment, as if astonished that the world goes on without him. In the next moment his breath catches and he's unimpressed again.

The relatives withdraw and I follow, leaving Margarita and Uncle alone together for the finale. We'll be back to offer benediction to the missionaries of EMS. We're not the only family set in motion by such a turn of events. We saunter outside to smoke and whisper beneath crackling electric wires.

# Chapter 19

## Aging and Other Bodily Conditions in
## This Life and Others

I don't grow old in one piece. Each part of me ages at a different rate. The women of my mother's generation aged in body long before face. I move forward in time, face-first. Actually, it's my neck that ages most rapidly, that which I thrust forward in risk. Perhaps my body perseveres because I'm never entirely at rest—subatomic particles collide within me, eroding, rearranging.

We're told the outward signs of aging can be staved off with surgical techniques. I remain skeptical even though I've seen some inspiring results. However, it doesn't always improve the appearance and often distorts and deforms. I don't wish to spend my dotage as a grotesque or cartoon figure. Well, that may happen anyway, but at least it will be of my own making.

As for the brain, physicists have found that in any closed unit, disorder (entropy) expands at the price of order (negentropy). I'm not sure how well this relates to me as I've always been fraught with disorder. I'm partial to the word "palimpsest." It's a word used to describe a characteristic of ancient manuscripts at a time when paper and parchment were difficult to come by. Writing material was specially prepared so that monks could write over the old manuscripts producing layers of material. This is how I feel about my mind. Though I have trouble remembering facts and events, they systematically overwrite older concepts and incidents, producing my current beliefs and persona. I'm a woman of many layers even though I've forgotten their precursory content. It involves a certain amount of trust to be who I am now. But who else would I dare to be?

~

## She Who Was Once

The people who speak to her are not great poets. They speak in simple sentences and use modest words. They do not attempt to communicate complex ideas, only everyday comments, greetings. No questions are asked beyond, "How are you?"

It's possible to go out, to walk, to take a meal with family though menus are no longer employed. "Spaghetti, hamburger." These are the foods she recognizes. Somehow "Diet Coke" is remembered. From one who often forgets to eat entirely, this is a quandary. How do such things become lastingly memorable? Didn't her mother make peanut butter sandwiches for school lunches, tea and toast on sick days? Wasn't there a diner with waitresses on roller skates serving graham cracker milkshakes, Jumpin' Jerry sundaes? Where are the memories of sweet potatoes, chocolate milk, apple dumplings, homemade bread warm from the oven? These are my memories, not hers. Hers are gone with yesterday's sunshine, a daughter's phone call, recognition of the road that gets you home from the drugstore. Soon these bits of memory will belong to someone else too.

She can't be trusted with car or money or stove. Unable to remember if she fed the dog, or where she put the soap, or how to use the phone, she recalls the necessary precautions when holding a baby. Her mind rambles, unable to attach itself to one voice, one task. It skims above meaning, not delving into a single word or phrase. Strings of words are broken and come tumbling down like snow about her. They form meaningless heaps to be kicked around, but moving through them is slippery, awkward. She doesn't dare try to handle them, combine them like snowballs because then they become frightening and take the form of a weapon, something thrown.

If she goes out alone, she might not be saved from mishap except by the kindness of strangers or strange kindnesses. Few outsiders are willing to slow down to her pace. Fifty-six is not old, not young, but fleeting. Numbers, letters, symbols for how the world works, waft on a wind that whirls such concepts beyond her.

My memories are on paper, written out in no particular order, for no good reason, collected in books. Daily, I practice the long intricate ritual of tai chi chu'an and the poem grandmother taught me as a child. When I can't remember where I put the keys or the movie becomes confusing or when I'm advised that I've told the same story before, I shudder, and hope that it isn't happening to me.

Perhaps she should be grateful that she can't remember her plan to grow old. But what is the present without past or future? It shifts in random spasms, unsteadily. When light changes, the vaguely familiar mutates and becomes Other. Then even the skin feels unfamiliar, old scars are meaningless, their tales lost. The flesh is vacant of all but bone; eyes are useless when they don't understand what they see. Soon even the moments of clarity will be forgotten. Soon she'll forget how to command the pieces of herself.

She cannot follow the stream of a story, but she can appreciate a rhythm, the colors of sunset, the harmony of song. Not a fallen woman, but a woman who is falling. She knows you're there when you hold her hand.

~

From the ropy veins on the back of my hands, you might think I'm part plant. It's true that my mother was a delicate flower but she was quite human. My father tortured himself into stoic states that were reminiscent of vegetation and he was rooted to one place like a weed We all have some traits of plant life though we're unmistakably animal. As my hair falls out, it's being replaced by feathers, soft, downy and multicolored. It's a bit bland in its present incomplete state, but I expect it to become quite spectacular and afford me the option of flying.

~

Cousin Charlotte loved Willy John. Willy John was tall and lanky, funny in a dry sarcastic way. He played the guitar and knew a lot about computers. He was not traditionally handsome, but had an overwhelming personality that unnerved some people. Charlotte couldn't resist the way he looked at her; she relished his touch.

Willy John had several minor medical issues. He walked with a knobby cane that he'd carved himself, his gait slow and unbalanced. He tired easily. He required periodic medical attention and occasionally had to be hospitalized. Charlotte sat by his bed worrying that he would never be able to go home again. Each time, he managed to rally. Each time, his condition got a little more obscure.

Charlotte looked at other people who'd overcome similar problems and wondered why Willy John hadn't. Willy John resented and bemoaned his fate. He joked about his condition, but demanded disabled parking permits and front-row seating at concerts and plays. He made faces to cheer Charlotte up.

This didn't make Charlotte feel any better. She came to believe she was a bad person, undeserving of Willy John and he encouraged this attitude. Willy John convinced Charlotte that she was a bad person if she thought about leaving him.

Being disabled doesn't always make you a nice person.

It took a long time and much self-control to step away and weaken the memory of him. There were times when she thought she might die. It was more than her heart, her whole life was broken.

Then one day another boy came along. Innis had a broken life also. He'd escaped from a home of turmoil and trouble. He carried with him worries about his small sister and brother but, shattered as he was, he could do nothing to help them. Sometimes two broken lives make a whole and Charlotte and Innis fell in love. They joined together and made a life. Sometimes a single life is enough for two people.

Charlotte and Innis had a child of their own and were happy until Innis was run over by a truck.

Charlotte didn't want little Lana to see her cry so she cried in the shower (for we know this is the best place to have a good cry without anyone knowing). She did this every day for months.

~

My mother isn't the only dead person that hovers about the living. Some Buddhists say that a soul hovers in limbo for at least a hundred years before it's reborn, but where exactly is Limbo? I often see my father or cousin Cora on a crowded street.

I imagine someday I might run across the reincarnation of my Seneca ancestor. I'm sure he'd be interested in meeting me, and fate would bring us together. When I worked in the Museum of Natural History, I handled each Seneca object I came across carefully in case it might have belonged to him. I didn't feel familiar energy from any the pieces that came through that place but I'm not discouraged. I've seen native powers at work and know their sense of history and humor. I'm confident that one day a message, or the person himself, will come to me.

Perhaps my daughter's daughter will give birth to this ancestor. Perhaps I'll meet him in a Starbucks or a Stop and Shop. You have to stay vigilant in order to bring about this kind of encounter. You may see yourself in an old photograph or illustration in a book or magazine at a flea market. You might read about some historical figure and recognize situations or people. You might recognize a place you've never been before—not just a room, a whole country.

~

IS IT POLITE TO BLOW KISSES TO THE DEAD?

~

IT'S RARE FOR GOOD GUYS TO DIE IN MOVIES OR BOOKS. ONLY RECENTLY, HAS IT BECOME MORE COMMON. THIS IS NOT TRUE IN LIFE.

~

We worry each time our children get sick. I used to pray that the sickness might be transferred to me; often it did.

My daughter had a friend that was born with an incurable illness. The medical dictionary said that the life expectancy of people with this disease was twenty. The little girl was nicknamed Feathers, because she was so light. My daughter could lift her in and out of the car. At school, the kids carried her up and down the stairs on a pillow. Feathers became lighter and lighter as the disease progressed. They carried her on class trips, to dances, and rock concerts.

I worried about the inevitable effect of Feathers' death on my daughter. I asked what she knew about the disease and was surprised that she'd done a lot of research and knew more about it than I did. I worried that Feathers would die while my daughter was away at college and Paige would be so distraught she wouldn't be able to finish school.

No matter how many times they tell us that it doesn't do any good to think about death—yours or anyone else's, that you can't control when or how it will happen, or its effect on you or anyone else—it's hard to ignore those thoughts entirely.

Feathers lived ten years beyond her twentieth birthday and when she died, you could lift her with one hand. In her lifetime she touched the hearts of hundreds of people and they all came to the funeral. Feathers' parents, quiet people, were overwhelmed. Her friends began a charity in Feathers' name and have continued to raise money for pillows and research.

Other than her disease, Feathers was an ordinary child. She made friends, got sent to the principal's office for talking in class, wore tee shirts with her favorite band's logo on them, fussed with her hair. But she's famous to a lot of people and many more will benefit from the funds raised in her name.

There are people who seek fame with every ounce of strength they have and they are forgotten as soon as they die. You can never tell what you might be famous for after you're gone. My cousin Leanor was famous for playing the spoons. Louis' Uncle Moe was famous for aggressively biting the ends off of cigars. Booger Carney was famous for...well, you can imagine.

Be careful about what you take credit for.

~

I'm famous (in a small way) for laundry. It's my favorite household task. I accumulate great piles of it, even though there are only two of us now. There's something soothing about the hum of washer and dryer. It's gratifying to put foul-smelling, stained clothing into a machine and take them out fragrant and sparkling, fold them carefully, and present them to someone. My family takes this for granted, but outsiders are suitably grateful when I do their laundry.

I even take pleasure in ironing. This was originally due to the Turner Movie Channel. Most people tune into a news network, but I looked to Ted's movies to lighten my mood. (Actually, I will watch most movies.) It's difficult to sit through an entire classic movie, action moved slowly in the early days of cinema and the story-lines are often hard to identify with. But a half hour here and forty minutes there—it's always a treat. I realize how beautiful Ingrid Bergman was, how intense Orson Wells was even in bad movies, and that Groucho Marx was once a young man. I admit to being irritated by Katherine Hepburn's self-assurance, and Joan Crawford's eyebrows. Greta Garbo was beautiful, but I don't get the impact of her as an actress. I marvel at Fred and Ginger. Have you seen *Moby Dick* lately? Was Shirley Temple really a child?

My all-time favorite actor is Charles Laughton. I find him totally engaging and when I happen upon one of his movies, I sit and watch it to the end, often long after I've finished ironing. He was always old. I wish Gracie Allen had made more movies. I wish they'd show her TV shows more often. She's agelessly clever and the funniest woman ever...

Louis and I are great fans of movies in general, but like books, I rarely remember much after I've seen them. I don't like car chases or extended fighting unless it's a martial arts movie, but then it's more of a dance, isn't it? I saw one Chinese movie where they fought while moving around on the rope-rigging of old sailing vessels. I like it when they swing long pigtails around to whip and entangle each other. I like it when they fly.

I remember when Mr. Turner decided to add color to classic black and white films. This brought about a huge protest and, as far as I can see, he's given up on this idea. Thank goodness. Some things are ludicrous in color.

The movies I've seen the most times in the theater are: *The Vikings* and Fellini's *Satyricon* (five times each). Movies I can always watch pieces of: *Star Wars*, *Apocalypse Now*, any Fellini movie, *Frida* (Don't you love the costumes?). I'm a little sick of *The Godfather*; it's always on.

Don't get me started on books.

~

I hope to be immortal in print one day. And, yes, me, Louis, the kids and our first dog appear in two "cult" films. I'm not good in front of a camera but I am better in color than black and white. It's not as easy as it looks. The photographer at Harlie's wedding told us to say "Thursday" rather than "cheese?"

"The dentist is running ninety minutes late." "Thursday." The girl ahead of you in the movie line invites three groups of friends to get in front of her. "Thursday." Ben & Jerry are discontinuing the flavor, peanut butter cup. "Thurs...Wait! What?"

~

When there's nothing on TV or you can't get to the movies, you can always look out the window to observe life. My father liked to sit at his kitchen window and watch squirrels jump from tree to tree. I'm happy I live in the city. This is the sort of thing I see out my window now:

Grey men with tool boxes appear across the street. They walk as if they were exhausted but it's only eleven o'clock in the morning. Perhaps they were out all night on an emergency call.

There are three enormously fat women and a man to match behind the grey men. His belt must be as long as I am tall. There's a silver-haired man wearing a leather jacket that's much too youthful for him. He carries a shopping bag and looks around guiltily. A young girl with tightly curled red hair done up like a topiary passes. Her step is bouncy. She's a waft of fresh air in this dreary street.

A pair of policemen walk by. They disappear into the deli. A young black man stops to write something on the back of an envelope. He may be a poet. He renders a satisfying click with his pen when he finishes, and smiles to himself.

Madness approaches. "Glory! Glory!" it calls, swelling through the street from a black Kia.

These people are familiar but I don't know any of them in this life. Some of them may be actors but they're not acting now. All of them are aging.

What sort of life passes by your window?

~

My Viking ancestors were rapists and pillagers. I don't want to meet them in this life unless they've reformed. Perhaps they've come back as farm animals or insects. Perhaps I have met them. Perhaps I've been saved from their clutches by the Lone Ranger. I hope they aren't reborn into my grandchildren or their children—unless, of course, they've learned their lesson.

~

On the day of Louis' Uncle Harry's funeral, the temperature began in the nineties. Each half hour it rose by one degree. Not a whisk of air moved. The burden of sun weighed on everyone. Sun and grief compressed them, made them small and heavy in their dark clothing.

The men driving the hearse got directions to the grave from a man in the main building of the cemetery, a building that looked like a bank. We wound our way through the flat and stark graveyard to an open grave. There we sat, waiting for a sister who'd apparently gotten lost. We discussed the service, commented on how hungry we were.

Louis had been asked to give a eulogy, which was strange as he barely knew his Uncle Harry and didn't particularly like him. I suggested that he refuse politely as he was generally not comfortable speaking in front of people, but he was determined not to let the family down. There was no one else capable. He'd sat up half the night scribbling, talking on the phone to various relatives who had stories about Harry. Behind us at the services, Harry's sister, Bella, sobbed unmercifully. She lived in New Jersey and hadn't seen Harry in two years. In their adult life, she'd only seen Harry on holidays and in the last few years Harry hadn't shown up for many of those. No one really knew what Harry's business was, only that he'd made and lost fortunes, that when he came to your house, small objects and cash would go missing.

When Louis stood up to speak, he froze, dropped his notes and scrambled to pick them up and put them in order. The silence of the crowd unnerved him further and he was unable to speak. He cleared his throat, croaked, and cleared his throat again. I had been studying chi gong and practicing faithfully. From my seat, I called on the spirits of the universe, and sent light and energy to Louis with all my might. Louis shook himself and began speaking. As he spoke, he became more and more confident. By the end of his speech the crowd was convinced that Uncle Harry, absent in spirit and virtue for years, was a man they all knew and loved.

In the car, while Louis stood outside accepting congratulations for his speech, I told the kids, then eleven and thirteen, what I had done. "Aw, Mom," they said skeptically, "You're so weird."

When Louis got in, we told him what a great job he'd done. "I didn't think you'd make it for a while, Dad," Harlie said.

"I didn't think I would either," Louis said. "Then all of a sudden, I got this wave of energy that carried me through. It was like something lifting me up, helping me breathe. It was weird."

The kids looked at me. "Mom is Yoda," Harlie whispered.

Bella finally arrived at the cemetery, 250 pounds of frazzle and fuss. She heaved herself out of the car and led the mourners to the grave without waiting for her long-suffering husband. Bella was in her glory, she was certain these people didn't know or care much for Harry; they were here for her.

All the mourners wore sunglasses; still, sun glinted off the polished stones in the cemetery and blinded them. None of the stones were older than ten years.

The gravesite smelled of fresh soil, a live scent at odds with the somber rite of death. Watching a coffin being lowered into a grave is a final act even when you have little connection with the person inside. We see ourselves going into the ground one day. The Rabbi was mercifully brief in the heat and Bella ceremoniously shoveled the first soil onto the coffin. She stood with arms folded over massive breasts and tears rolling down her cheeks while the other mourners added their shovelfuls.

In the car, out on the highway, we discussed *Star Wars*. Louis had lost the thread of the plot in part II and III, and Harlie tried patiently to explain about the Rebellion and the Empire, Luke and Leia.

At Bella's house, the kids played video games upstairs in their cousin's room. Bella got the attention she thought she deserved and everyone admired her collection of painted rocks. As usual, enough food was consumed to support a small country. This would go on for days.

~

There's nothing like death to make people feel alive.

~~

They came with guns and machines and dug up sacred objects from grave sites. No one dared stop them. They weighed the gold and measured the gems, but didn't bother to learn the stories. The objects were sold to wealthy housewives. They were hung above living room couches and on dining room walls; they were placed on coffee tables and mantels. They presided over lives that were very different than the lives they had been created to protect.

Some of the exposed children were affected. They chanted in strange languages and performed ancient dances. The parents took them to doctors who gave them medicine, but it was not the "old medicine." Some of the behavior stopped but the curse persisted. Since the stories have been lost, we can't know the ending. The people in the villages remain poor.

~

On the morning of September 11, 2001, I was out walking my dog in our Chelsea neighborhood. When I came in my husband said, "Come look at this. A plane flew into the World Trade Center."

"Well, they must have been really tanked," I told him. "It's a perfect day, not a cloud in the sky."

My children had finished college and were living at home again. Paige went off to her new job downtown.

No sooner had she left the house than the second plane hit. I ran down the street looking for her, but she was gone. Harlie was home and had his TV on; we watched in horror. Paige was back within a few minutes. "The subway's not working; there are no cabs," she said. "How am I going to get to work?"

She tried to call her boss but the phones were affected and worked only intermittently for the next few days.

It was an odd scenario, first sirens, noise, phones silent for hours then ringing, hysteria, waiting. Refugees (friends and acquaintances who couldn't get out of the city once it was closed off) gathered at our house. We watched TV, went out into the street to see the smoke after the towers fell. Shopped for food, zombie-like, at the mostly empty grocery store.

Then there was a dreadful stillness. Trains had been stopped below 23rd Street, so there wasn't the usual white noise in our neighborhood (21st Street, Ninth Avenue). The phones stopped working. Sirens and traffic had stopped. TVs were tuned reverently low. Refugees headed home mutely, and lines of people trudged up Ninth Avenue. Covered in white dust like zombies, they didn't speak, we didn't dare speak to them.

The next day, Harlie and I made sandwiches at Chelsea Market to be sent to the workers at Ground Zero. Local stores and restaurants donated food. I recommended that they not use mayonnaise as it spoils rapidly in heat, a lesson I learned from participating in protests in the sixties. Late in the afternoon they told us not to come back, that major restaurants and caterers would be supplying food to rescue workers. As it turned out, there was plenty of work to do but no one to rescue.

Emergency triage centers were idle.

On the second day, the wind changed and for five hours the stench of destruction, death and fear permeated our Chelsea neighborhood. There were few cars, but at sunset one passed our house. It was spray-painted with the words, "READY 4 WAR." I was sitting on the stoop and a man yelled out from it, "Don't be sad; kill an A-rab." This event left me shaking and dazed in anxiety. I was more frightened at that moment than I had been the day before.

Everyone lit candles and consoled each other, strangers helped strangers. We studied the photos of the missing, which were everywhere. The local fire department was flooded with flowers, candles, gifts of food. It looked like a Korean fruit market.

At the medical examiner's office, where I served food, thousands of cards and notes came from all over the world, pictures drawn by school children, banners. People from other parts of the country used their vacations to come help out. A building on Fourteenth Street was donated for a few weeks and we gave toys to victim's children for the holiday. Besides toys, thousands of stuffed bears had been donated. Each bear had a handwritten note attached, a note of sympathy from mothers, fathers, children. Every child that came got a bear and was allowed to choose three toys, three being a magic number—but there was no magic to be had in the gloom of those days.

We were given gloves, donated by the manufacturer, to keep our hands warm in the unheated building. The workers downtown had no protection from the heat of "the pile" or the polluted air that permeated the area.

~

I know the name of God. He signed a tree in my hometown; I used to see it on my way to school when I was a child. It's: "Buddy K."

That tree, the one creation that God was proud enough to sign, has been cut down.

~

Saturday we had cake, dark Mexican chocolate with a sigh of mint. It was baked in huge sheets, enough for the whole wedding party and all the relatives and friends attending the wedding. Afterwards we couldn't remember the cut of the bride's dress or which songs the band played. We forgot the sadness we'd felt for those who were missing from the happy occasion. We could only remember the caress of melting chocolate in warm mouths and the kiss of mint.

~~

In the face of death, we cling to life and chocolate.

~

There are some deaths that we relive repeatedly. How many times have we seen the World Trade Center fall? The Kennedys shot? Each year there's a spontaneous memorial for John Lennon in Central Park. These deaths were so shocking that we must experience them again and again to convince ourselves that they really happened and to deaden the pain of the experience.

Gram Little used to mark her life by the deaths she'd experienced. "The year before dad died…" "Three years after

Walter died…" Historical events were attached to the deaths of family and friends. At 110, she'd seen a lot of death.

My Manx grandmother planned for her own death by attaching our names to her belongings and announcing that she didn't want her body brought back to Pennsylvania to be put in the "family plot." She was happy to be buried in Miami with Nigel Skifflington. I can't blame her for this. It's quite possible, despite the serenity of that Appalachian country cemetery, that the graves will one day sink into an abandoned mine. It happens every day in that area. I hope it doesn't happen to my grandfather as he spent his life in mines and deserves to have his remains rest for eternity in ground that's firm and stable (as much as possible). Then again, he may wish to dwell in the mines with the ghosts of his fellow workers.

We don't always get what we deserve.

# Chapter 20

## Jumping for Light

One morning when I took Puppet out for her walk, we were greeted by a band of yellow police tape, a covered lump, and a crowd on the street in front of the building next to us. "What's this?" I asked the policeman.

"Jumper," he said.

This is the conversation I overheard between another policeman and some neighbors:

A woman identifying herself as Mrs. Fieldstone said, "There were three distinct pops, Detective Mullen," as she stared at the body on the sidewalk.

"Followed by a low rumble," a Miss Smidtke added. "Like an earthquake." (Miss Smidtke said she lived on the first floor.)

"More of a knocking," said a Mr. Ortiz.

"No. No. I was on the roof," Mr. Wilson, the super, waved his arms. "Just a clatter, then splat, she hit the ground.

The radio in the police car crackled and Detective Mullen mumbled something to the Sergeant.

"Everyone over here," the Sergeant ordered. "I'll take statements one at a time."

"How's it going?" The dispatcher barked over the radio. "Oh, this is a real hoot," Mullen answered.

I heard later that an old woman who lived on the twelfth floor just opened her window, unlocked the iron gate, and jumped. The "pops" were parts of her body hitting the building as she fell. No one seemed to know her name. Some people thought she was a man.

This wouldn't have been the case in my small hometown. Everyone would have known who she was and the story of her distress would have passed from one side of town to the other. Would this have made her life better? Possibly. It may have made it worse.

Surely, someone would have offered friendship or help. If they had known...

~

Many people favor small towns and country living; they would never choose to spend their lives in a large, noisy, dirty, dangerous city. My old friends and relatives can't understand why I would do such a thing. Louis' family lives in the suburbs and they can't fathom it. It's not easy to explain and you can never understand it by just visiting the city. Visiting is entirely different than being a part of it.

I only know that I used to lie awake at night, listening for a train whistle to break the silence, and wonder what the world was doing without me. I didn't want to read the news in the paper or watch TV; I wanted to see people, ordinary people going about their business. I wanted to listen in to their conversations. You might feel that a walk in the country is blissful, but I'd rather drift through city streets, listening, watching. I've never heard the trees talk but I've heard secrets on the street and in buses and trains. Watching clouds move slowly across a clear sky only makes me impatient. I find myself wishing for a storm, thunder and lightning, spinning ozone, something I can get lost in.

What I miss about being in the country is stars. The city lights are so bright that we rarely see stars, except in the Planetarium. On vacations, I bask in the night skies.

I'm not ready to join them, though, not prepared to have my soul float to the dome of the world or to be gathered up by the Sky Holder. I'm still too attached, too comfortable in my place on this planet.

~

A Bodhisattva is an enlightened being that chooses to come back after death to help others reach enlightenment, a soul that's too "attached" to humanity to leave it as it is, a compassionate being that wants all creatures to achieve Nirvana. I don't fit into this category as I can't see how I could be of any help to anyone (though I have been, but mostly by accident).

I have had fleeting moments of Enlightenment (haven't we all?), but I don't expect any of them to become permanent in this life or for many more lives to come. It's possible that my most profound "fleeting moment" was in childhood and I'll never have another—in this life.

~

Louis' Great Aunt Nettie didn't want to go to her husband's funeral. "I hated the old goat. It was fifty-eight years of Hell living with him. Good riddance to bad times."

"But he's the father of your children. He gave you everything you wanted. You had a good life," Louis' mother told her.

"I had a rotten life. He owed me jewelry and trips, fur and fancy houses for making my life miserable. I coulda married a nice Italian boy. I shoulda married Vinnie. My momma made me marry a Jew and look how it turned out. I shouldn't a listened."

"Nettie, you have nice children, a nice home and plenty of money. You're set for life."

"Yea, some life. I'm seventy-eight years old. My eyes don't work; I have arthritis, high blood pressure; my back is killing me and my feet are swollen. Where am I going? Is there a nice Italian boy out there for me now? Maybe I should call up that Jake Law fella."

"Jude Law. Jude, like 'Hey, Jude'—you know, the Beatles song."

"He's got Beatles? That figures, all the good ones get those sex diseases."

"Nettie, please, not in front of children."

"Children halfta learn. How'r they gonna learn? Listen to me, children; don't listen to your momma. Watch out for diseases."

I liked Nettie. Her husband **was** an old goat. Unfortunately, Nettie didn't get to live it up for long after he died. Her daughter put her in "assisted living" for her own "good," and she ended her days playing Mah Jong and watching game shows. She was, however, able to cause a few more stinks at family gatherings and I think that pleased her.

It's important not to waste too much of your life putting up with things and people you don't really like. It's too late for Nettie. How about you?

~

Why do we drink coffee before and after funerals? Is it to get the blood moving, to make us feel alive? Or is it because our funerals are basically boring and you might fall asleep and embarrass yourself? If you can't prove your Viking and Seneca heritage, can you have a funeral that incorporates customs of both in order to entertain your mourners, give them something to talk about?

I can hear Nettie say, "What the Hell."

~

One of the arguments for cremation is that we're taking up too much space dead and alive. Not only are there more of us and some becoming increasingly obese, but we demand an inordinate amount of goods and paraphernalia during the course of our existence. Much of this we didn't want to begin with, but were talked into thinking we need it by clever advertising. Much of it is ultimately relegated to the status of garbage, which grows in piles that take up more space and emit foul odors and gases. We claim that we need space to breathe, yet most animals huddle together in packs and prides. Only wind and sky make excellent use of space by not filling it up.

A great many people are waiting for a "savior" to rescue them and/or all of us. Some people believe such a being has already been here and will return to complete the mission. Why would such a being leave and then return? Forgot the keys? Left the oven on? Maybe a vacation was needed; it is an awfully big job.

# Chapter 21

## Nature (the world's)

Fall is Road Kill season. All the little animals scamper around looking for food and end up being squashed by cars. Their bleeding furry bodies litter the roads in the countryside at a time when people go to view the colorful foliage. Despite this, fall is my favorite season. I don't like heat and I'm always relieved when it subsides. I don't dislike winter; cold is much easier to deal with than heat. You can always put on more clothes and blankets. A cold wind can whip life into the most lethargic person. The breath is visible, the body inspired to move. Blustery winter days can be trying, but Autumn is perfection in temperature and color. It brings about an attitude of balance. A certain seriousness about "digging in" is required—amid riotous color that encourages inspiration. People take light-hearted trips to view foliage and are greeted by the aforementioned hunks of bloody fur and crushed bone—frivolity meets reality.

On the other hand, heat is the adversary of thought and movement in those of us whose ancestors came from cool climates. There's little you can do about heat; air conditioning is often too extreme and pollutes the air with unnatural chemicals and noises. It offers a false sense of stimulation.

It's a fact that certain mutable matter is preserved best in a cool climate, though there are people who are genetically predisposed to living in tropical environments. These people are dark-skinned and hardy. For the the pale and wan, refrigeration is key in staying fresh.

My cousin Jane moved to Florida when she turned thirty. She was looking for "the good life." Jane was divorced and childless, annoyed by her freedom. She took a waitress job at the House of Fish in Wakeville, Florida.

Personally, I love being a waitress. I did it all through college and it might be the best job I ever had. You're not stuck behind a desk; you get to meet a lot of people who are out to eat and therefore usually in a good mood. (You should resist the urge to take a waitress job at a very ritzy place, despite the fact that you might make better tips. Customers who frequent these places are largely business people and rich people with "issues" who eat out too often to appreciate the experience. Better to work in a resort restaurant, small café, or family place.)

Jane's place of occupation was an on-the-water, resort-type restaurant that attracted a lot of retired people, middle-class people who ate early and left (mostly) decent tips.

Still, Jane was unhappy. She married three men in seven years (sequentially). It was the middle one, George, that everyone in the family loved, but he didn't last long. Jane ended up with a sweaty ex-Virginian with hair plugs. She stays at home, tends her garden, plays cards with the girls, and has taken up collecting painted rocks (another one, what is this?)

Jane professes to have a busy rewarding life, but spends an inordinate amount of time complaining. She finds flaws in her friends and acquaintances. She can't stand being around children or pets. She finds fault with her local stores and restaurants. She doesn't like movies and rarely leaves her Florida home. Jane has tuned out, turned off, and dropped in.

I think it's the heat.

Give me cool air, falling leaves and road kill any day.

~

Of course, you can never count on anything being what it's expected to be all the time.

Even stillness isn't still. At those times when I wake in the middle of the night, I imagine myself packed inside stillness like fine china in foam. But the air still vibrates slightly. I think the vibration's caused by my own breath so I hold it in. I'm perfectly still, not tense, but waiting. The vibration persists, ever so faintly. It comes from something greater and won't be stifled.

Long after someone's gone there's a hum, a scent, a whisper. Energy is not lost but transformed.

~

Walk in the woods. There's nothing clean about nature. It gets on your shoes, underneath your fingernails, in the folds and crevices. It's sticky. It pricks and can cause infection. It might cause rashes, allergies.

It teems with creatures that are never still unless they're preparing to attack. It's there to remind us that we're small and absolutely not in control. It's there to loom over us and seduce us with misleading signs. Don't believe anyone who says they can read the signs of nature. One day they'll be duped. No one is beyond the power of nature.

Especially human beings.

# Chapter 22

## What We Love About...and Questions

Things I've never done that I have no desire to do: drink a Diet Coke, skydive, run a company, be on a reality show, go to the North Pole, meet George Bush, build a house, kill anything.

Things that I still want to do: everything else.

~

Louis' Uncle Sid lives in the suburbs and rides a train into the city every day for work. He works at a dress company on Seventh Avenue. Seventh Avenue used to be a bustling, exciting place. Fortunes were made. It's not like that today as most garments are made in other countries.

Uncle Sid was once very rich and he still is, by most standards, but he doesn't make enough money to suit his wife and children's needs. His children, though grown, still expect a great deal of monetary assistance. Sid should retire and enjoy his remaining years, but he wouldn't know what to do with himself.

So he takes the train each day to a near-death industry. The streets are no longer crowded with trucks and men pushing racks of clothing and piece goods. Many of the old structures have been converted to residential buildings. Sid remembers when they were sweatshops and showrooms. He wonders what happened to all the mice and roaches, the rats that overran the neighborhood in the past.

On the train Sid rides, there are seats that face both ways. Sid likes to ride backward on the train. He says you may never quite know where you are but at least you can be certain of where you've been. He says that the ride always changes, new buildings go up, old ones come down. For this reason, when you ride backward, the present isn't an issue. The future is a mystery; you round a bend and the past is gone, a distant memory.

I wonder about Uncle Sid. Does he ever turn his head to catch a glimpse of the future? Where does he look when the train stops? What's he afraid of?

One thing we can all count on: the future is rushing into the present as rapidly as the present rushes into the past; we're all riding that train. Perhaps this is why it's so difficult to remain in the present, as the gurus tell us we should do. What we don't know, that Sid knows, is what happens when we get off the train; if, like me, you believe in reincarnation—how is it, that when we get on again, we get on at a different stop?

When Gram Little was a child, people rode in horse-and-buggies; before she died, she saw men walk on the moon (though she didn't believe it was true). I'm very fond of trains, a little leery of horses, and have no desire to ride a government vehicle into space. My preferred method of transport is my own feet.

My dad was very fond of boats. This is probably a consequence of his Viking heritage. But he rarely got to ride in one. I admit to being enchanted with the idea of the sea, but experience violent motion sickness in boats.

~

An endearing fact about Louis: He's hoping for a sequel to *Thelma and Louise.*

~

When Louis and I were first married, we lived in an apartment next to an older woman we saw infrequently. The woman was pleasant, grandmotherly. She "did the books" for "a nice young man in the importing business." The neighbors on the other side, a snobby gay couple, had noisy parties every Saturday night that always ended with a loud, sing-along rendition of "Baby You're the Bottom, I'm the Top."

The old woman spent her evenings with her bird, Blue, until he died unexpectedly. We ran into her carrying Blue out in a shoe box one Sunday morning. "I'm going to throw him off the Staten Island Ferry," she said. "Ashes to ashes, dust to dust, air to water."

We offered our condolences.

"You get used to death at my age," she sighed. "Life goes on. We had a good run, Blue and I." She seemed very composed and resigned.

When she died, a nephew came to clear out her apartment. The old woman had saved all her nail clippings (and possibly Blue's) in jars that she stored in the linen closet. He found sixteen boxes of Cheerios, and nine sets of souvenir glasses from Niagara Falls, a place he was certain his aunt had never been.

Friends of the gay couple next door moved into her apartment and painted the whole thing white (the Chinese color of death). They were much more hospitable than the couple on the other side of us, and invited us to all their parties. However, we'd bought a place on Tenth Street and moved out two months later.

I'm careful to dispose of my own nail clippings so no one can find them, just as I'm careful who I tell my true name to.

~

You have to be cautious in today's world without becoming obsessed. It's a delicate balance. Death, as the old woman said, is a part of life and you can't allow it to diminish your time of living. There are too many things that do this already.

Take for instance, reading a newspaper. This is done every day by most people. Newspapers are harbingers of bad news in juxtaposition with appeals for living: atrocities sandwiched between ads for expensive footwear, mood-elevating drugs, and appearance enhancing cosmetics. In such a setting, the obituaries are a ray of sunshine: affectionate profiles, achievements of the great and small among us.

Today on the island of Aaght Aaghe in the Greater Salent Islands, 327 people were killed during elections. Nine American soldiers were killed "keeping the peace." Plans for the assassination of the coach of the Owosso Owls were found in a basement in Grand Rapids. A bank built in 1829 was bulldozed to make way for the Napolean Colorado MegaMall, which will be anchored by a 30,000 foot PayLater store. And two members of the President's cabinet have been indicted for taking bribes from the company responsible for the oil spill off of Virginia Beach.

While in the obituaries the inventor of the harmonimer, the world's most beautiful instrument, "caught a stroke." Red spindle cells caught up with the artist who drew and wrote the

*The Planet Pete Pea Shootin' Pony* series of children's books. And a woman in Straw Pump died in her sleep. She'd raised fifteen kids (five of them her own), ran a health center, collected money and clothing for eight charities and, yes, collected painted rocks.

Every time Gram Little heard bad news, she claimed that forces were gathering for the Apocalypse; for her, every day there were more signs that pointed to the end of the world. She, of all people, should have known better. Atrocities are not a new development in this world. A good Apostle should have known that there were scores of atrocities in the Bible: a flood that wiped out the entire planet except for those saved by Noah, Lot's wife, Babylon, the Ammonites, the Philistines, the Syrians, the Egyptians…We've fought a slew of wars and who's exempt from the blame for them? Who hasn't experienced violence and mayhem? China, Japan, Nigeria, Darfur, Cambodia, Somalia, Guatemala, Iraq, Afghanistan? America? I could name every country in the atlas. No one's exempt.

I prefer to remember Gram Little's apple dumplings than her predictions of doom. In the same way, some days I skip the news and read the obituaries to cheer myself up.

My Manx grandmother thought beyond death by attaching the names of friends and relatives to her possessions. "This ceramic frog is for Felicity" "This awful broach is for Estelle." This is what we do when we make a will.

Some people think that the BIG QUESTION is "What does it all mean?" In my experience the meaning keeps changing. It means different things to different people at different times. Sometimes things are entirely meaningless.

What if everybody tried not to be mean? Now, that would mean something.

# Chapter 23

## Legends

The founder of the Isle of Man had a reputation for magic. He traveled the Celtic world in many forms. He had a horse that could travel swiftly over land and sea, impregnable armor, a cloak of invisibility, a magic sword called "the Answerer" and, most important, a fairy branch with nine golden apples that made music when shaken and brought forgetfulness of sorrow and woe.

This is a legend worth having.

I didn't have anyone to teach me the legends of the Senecas, but I imagine they have their brave warriors with powerful gifts.

Choose any of the legends of the world to dance to and make offerings to. Become a legend yourself.

~

### The Goddess of Outen

Somewhere in the debris of the Lesser Sunda Islands in the Indian Ocean, lies a tiny, but lush, island known as Outen. The inhabitants are a mixture of Dyak outcasts and lost pirate crews, people that even the outlaws of Australia refused to take in. Through centuries of isolation and mixed breeding, they developed their own civilization and racial genre.

They are small and brown. Most have shocking orange hair

that seems to grow straight out from the head, a trait inherited from one extremely robust renegade from the pirate contingent. These rogue outcasts, deprived of civilized influence and left to their own devices, flourished on the little island and evolved an extremely good nature as evinced in the gentle eyes of their descendants. They retain the cleverness of pirates and dexterity of the Dyak, and they move about their daily occupations with the languid rhythm of the waves that lick their shore.

Among the residents of Outen, there was once a woman named Anathema; the old ones call her the Goddess of Caducity, and worship at her sacred mountain. This sacred "mountain" in the vernacular of such a small island, is little more than a hill, but it seems to attract all the lightning that befalls the area. (Scientists speculate the existence of a metallic vein of some kind.) Anathema's mountain is covered with briar bushes, which accounts for the many tears in her clothing. She is taller than the general population, and bone-thin; a build never prized by the Outen. A missing arm is replaced by a thick briar branch, laden with bits of refuse caught out of the air. One eye is replaced by a button which, when tapped, enhances her brain and stimulates her thought process. In her frazzled gray hair she keeps snacks and writing materials. Despite her appearance, not even the children are frightened of her.

They say that when the Goddess was a young woman, she captained a pirate ship out of Doubtless Bay, that she watched her crew tortured and eaten in Palau Uwi before escaping to Borneo and falling in love with a mortal headhunter possessed of many brave souls. Together they settled in Outen and when her mortal lover died, she went to the mountain to dwell with the lightning.

Because the lightning is drawn to Anathema's mountain, the people believe all lost things are attracted to her; and because

the briars hold what is blown by the wind, they believe all that
is missed is in her keeping. The women bake bread in the shape
of lost people and possessions. They mark it with stones, speak
charms over it, and offer it to the Goddess. The men keep
the mountain paths cleared so the lost things can make their
way to her. Together, they perform ritual dances in intricate
interlacing patterns and pray at the foot of the mountain.
The Outen do not pray for the return of their lost things,
however. That would be heresy in virtue of their history. They
pray to the Goddess to respect and care for what has been lost.
They ask forgiveness for their attachment to the person or thing
that is missing. Then, if the Goddess deems the supplicant truly
pious, she will offer something in return. For the Outens believe
that loss is necessary to stimulate development, that we gain
ten-fold what we lose, that those who lose abundantly are most
sacred. They revel in privation, give thanks for bereavement.
In the 250 years since Outen was settled, they have periodically
been plagued by developers and pillaged by merchants. The
Outens welcomed these vandals with open arms. It is even said
that one particularly ruthless merchant was sacrificed to the
Goddess, who then butchered and dressed the carcass, grilled the
meat, and delivered it to the village in order to stave off the
famine that he'd caused.
"Just as the Goddess sustained the loss of her loyal crew and was
given the love of the many souls that inhabited the headhunter;
just as she lost him and was given the very lightning from the
sky; just as her appendages were lost and replaced by more
useful contrivances, so shall we gain by our losses. Amen."

~

Louis' family legend has to do with a Great Aunt who stayed

in Russia when the rest of his family came to America. Aunt Kaza was a mathematician who worked on "secret government projects" (so they believe). She wasn't permitted to have any contact with her family for more than thirty years. After the Reagan administration, when the Russians reorganized, she moved to Canada but couldn't get a job since she didn't speak the language. She had to move back to Russia, and no one ever heard from her again. Nevertheless, the family is convinced that she's behind all the great technical advances of the Russians in the Twentieth Century. Who's to say they're wrong? Their only other claim to fame is a niece that's often mistaken for Lindsey Lohan.

~

I'd like to meet the "legend" who convinced people to buy and collect painted rocks.

~

Of all the great screen legends, I'd like to meet Gracie Allen. I know she wasn't in many movies, I can think of only two: *The Gracie Allen Murders* and *Hawaii*. In *Hawaii*, she stole the show from Eleanor Powell, which wasn't easy to do. I still watch her TV program when ever it's shown. George and Gracie must have been a fun couple to hang out with. I'd be disappointed to find out she was any different off the screen.

~

My cousin Hallard lives in an underground house in Texas. Hallard built this house himself because he lives in a "tornado lane." It seems to me that he might have moved to another spot since he works for the electric company and there are electric companies everywhere, but I suppose electric workers are urgently needed in tornado lanes. You couldn't build an underground house in my hometown without hitting an old mine shaft.

Hallard enjoys mowing his roof and reading his junk mail. He found a wife thanks to an online dating service.

A life under the ground is not the same as being buried.

~

I'm very fond of scuba diving, despite my proclivity for getting sea sick. I haven't been diving for many years, but Louis and I used to go to Belize once a year for this purpose. The dive master would tell everyone that "Felicity will be the first one in the water when we get to the site and the last one to get out of the water. Allow her to sit in the middle of the boat and do not block her view of the horizon. Do not engage her in conversation if she feels that she can't talk."

Once I'm under the water, I'm fine. I love the feeling of weightlessness and the sound of my own breathing. I may have been a fish in another life. Here's another story of a brush with death:

We were diving with a group of people and one of the women had a shark phobia. She talked about her fear of sharks continuously; it was very irritating. This was a woman who wore pantyhose beneath her wetsuit, and we were forced to watch her struggle into and out of them, talk about irritating! On the way back from a dive we spotted a school of dolphin. We grabbed our goggles and snorkels and jumped off the boat to swim with them. The dive master assured this woman that sharks never swim with dolphins. I was following a particularly graceful fish when the woman swam past me and announced that she'd seen a shark. Yea, right, I thought and dove down after the dolphin. Then something very large came from behind and swam past me—a shark! A whale of a shark, maybe twelve, fifteen feet long! Divers see harmless nurse sharks often and this was definitely **not** a nurse shark. This was "Jaws." A killer. There's nothing you can do in such a situation; survival isn't up to you, it's a matter of fate. The shark swam straight ahead as if on a mission. He paid no attention to me (which is odd since I don't look anything like a dolphin or anything else he might have been accustomed to seeing in the water).

I bobbed up to the surface and swam back to the boat as fast as I could. Everyone else was swimming madly. When I got to the ladder a huge (and hysterical) guy pushed me off in order to get onto the boat first.

It took everyone some time to calm down and I'll bet the shark-woman's never gone back into the water. I was the only one who got close enough to touch it—not that I considered reaching out for the thing. Perhaps the shark recognized me as a friend from another life.

If I'm not reincarnated into this world next time around, I hope there's another world that's like being underwater—but without sharks.

~

At family gatherings my cousins would inevitably mention Alice. If the aunts heard, they would shake their heads and hold fingers to their lips in the sign for quiet.

"Why can't we talk about Alice?" I'd ask when I was a kid. The cousins would take me aside and whisper, "Because she isn't married."

This confused me. I wasn't married—but I was a child; they

talked about me all the time, right in front of me as if I wasn't there. The cousins were older and they weren't married; no one hushed you for talking about them. When we were all together Alice was never invited or allowed to be spoken of. I'd never seen the mysterious Alice.

I found out later it was because Alice had a baby and had refused to "give it up." In those days it was a horrible thing to be an unmarried mother. Things have changed, even in my family.

In Louis' grandfather's day, if you married a non-Jew, you'd be dead to the family. That's not true today either. Both of my children married non-Jews and we have a fine time celebrating each other's holidays together. It's great to have so many holidays, each with its own traditions and food.

It's a strange impulse to consider someone dead when they're alive, especially when there are people who wish they were dead and people who allow certain significant parts of them to die, like emotions...

~

At our house we always have cake on May sixth for Willie Mays' birthday. Willie is very important to Louis. Willie is a living legend.

Pick your own legend and bake a cake.

~

To my knowledge, there's only one distant relative that ever admitted to being gay in my family. He and his partner are growing old happily. There are several very unhappy members of the family who should admit to something.

~

Mrs. Lin was not a motherly person. She berated all her students relentlessly. Still, we all attended her classes faithfully because she had a lot to teach us. She taught us about stillness and movement; she taught us the dance of the universe. It's a discipline we all continue to work at, one that necessitates many teachers.

Had you asked me, I would have said that Mrs. Lin was a very tall and dignified woman. Once she took us to see a performance of Balinese dancing. A great crowd of people exited the theater after the presentation and I couldn't find Mrs. Lin. Finally, I spotted her in the crowd, at least a foot shorter than anyone around her.

Height is an illusion, dignity is not.

At Mrs. Lin's memorial (she would never have allowed her students to see her dead), people stood and told stories about her. Her students were mature and poised, not given to emotion like the Apostles of the Little family. Each one began their story with the words, "I was Mrs. Lin's worst student because…"

~

In one life I was pushed off a cliff into a great abyss.

In another life I was a fish.

In many other lives Louis and I have been together. There are other people I recognize. Some I don't know in this life. I see them on the street; they see me, our eyes connect but we don't acknowledge our connection. Once I met a dog who recognized me; he was happy to confirm the bond between us.

Perhaps in another life I'll be a rock that someone painted

and I'll be loved and protected by a collector. Perhaps I'll end up being a rock in this life.

Most everyone in my lineage has "gone on." Only some distant cousins and their children remain but I don't keep in touch with them.

Louis has more living relatives than I, but they're dwindling.

*Louis can't be Jay*

# Chapter 24

## This Is the Way Young Boys Fight:

They stand in their uniforms and try not to think about how uncomfortable their feet feel in their heavy boots. They try not to think about the heat (or the cold). They try to think about a girl back home or a movie star but sometimes they can only remember their mother. They try not to think about the girl they saw on the street yesterday, or her hungry child. They don't really think but if they did, they'd think about food or a warm bed (even if they never had one). If they were to think about what they were doing in a strange place, they might remember employment or welfare offices, or boredom, a different boredom than they feel now. When they had time to think before—they thought about a future, how training (that they couldn't afford themselves) would get them a good job, or how the military would send them to school, or about how they'll be better off when they get back.

They don't know if what they are is brave or scared but we know it's both. They've never been in a situation so real before—even though they thought where they'd been was real. Something in their body spins, like a little tornado, it might make them dizzy and confused or it might spin out the cobwebs and make everything clear.

It might take away all their feelings or it might dump feelings on them that they've never had and can't understand. Their body tingles with it.

Sometimes they feel like they're in a movie.

Sometimes they feel like they're in a box.

They know who their friends are. They're not so sure about their enemies.

## This Is the Way Young Boys Die:

In faraway places like deserts or jungles. When they're afraid or when they're relaxed. When they don't expect it. When they have very little time left before they go home; when they have a lot of time left; when they just got there. Sometimes among friends; always among enemies. Quick or agonizingly slow. In pieces or with most of their limbs intact (as opposed to those who come back without all their pieces). In pieces after they come back.

Their names are written on memorials.

# Chapter 25

## Life Among The Living

### The Daughter

Once I had this baby girl and she was very beautiful and seemed so delicate. I thought, what'll I do with a baby girl? How will I keep her safe? I put her in a cushy box but she climbed out and broke all the eggs and got dirty and stood on the table and sang as loud as she could. So I bought her cowboy boots to wear with her nightgown and traded the box for a horse. When she fell off the horse, she just bounced but she had the most fearsome chickenpox of anyone in the history of the world.

She taught me how to stand on my head. We taught each other how to be brave. She says many wise things. Here's one of my favorites: "So much milk, not enough flakes," or is it the other way around?

### Walking With the Living

Louis and I walk Paige down the aisle as we walked Harlie several years before. Harlie's daughter, Audri scatters flower petals. As expected, she eats some of them and cries when she's told not to. My dauther-in-law walks behind the sister of Paige's new husband.

The room is filled with friends, new in-laws, surviving relatives, memories and ghosts. Paige has a handkerchief embroidered by Gram Little sewn into her wedding dress.

Sometime before the ceremony, M plays a trick, despite the fact that it's not her trickster season. We hear the panting of a dog that isn't there. Someone steps in something that resembles coal dust; the newlyweds receive a heartfelt gift from an anonymous giver and an ugly vase from a relative south of Pittsburgh. I offer them the gold-trimmed glasses M received for her wedding, but they have no more use for them than I or my mother had.

New people enter our lives—friends, children—some may be recognizable from other lives.

There will be dogs.

## Grandmothering
### (on the occasion of my son's first Father's Day)

I had this baby once, a boy baby who didn't sleep more than twenty or thirty minutes at a clip. When he was awake he wanted company, which I wasn't happy about at first, but then he thought I was way cool and he was eminently fascinating. So we stayed up together for years and when he started to become  a man, he finally went to sleep. I'd lost the habit of sleep, but I let him rest. When he woke up he looked for a wife and found one who was smart and curvy and they made this little person who could stay up with me sometimes. I teach her good stuff like how to make a guppy face, and do the Boston Monkey, and recite "Swinging on the Gate." I will always say "Yes" and "You win." (Ok, the "yes" thing may not always work out.) I will buy her frivolous footwear and soften peanut butter in the microwave to put on her ice cream.

## The Baby

They say that the baby looks like my son but I don't see it. All my babies looked like Alfred Hitchcock in profile, "Good evening." Never having met Mr. Hitchcock, I can't be accused of bearing his children and they didn't look a bit like him when they grew up.

"The baby" doesn't want to look like anyone but herself. Though born in a big city, she spits like a hillbilly (Appalachian American). She's amazingly intelligent, watchful, even at a young age.

I'm expecting grandmotherly wisdom to kick in any moment but instead, feel I'm regressing, becoming stupider, more childish.

~

A Possible Future:

Before my skin turned grey and my eyes dulled, there was a sparkle to both. I had fine long legs but never used any of these attributes to advantage. I was quiet and mousey. Now that everything's gone to ruin, I've grown loud, demonstrative, garish in my dress and attitude. I'm using my dotage as an excuse to misbehave and wish I'd done it much sooner. Misbehavior is wasted on the young and unappreciative. Whereas I can be kindly to those I deem worthy, I revel in making the unworthy squirm. I'm amused by their anger and frustration.

It's diabolical what an old woman can get away with. For instance, I eat what I wish in the grocery store. I look the produce man right in the eye and say, "these grapes are sour." I give advice to strangers. "Lose that joker, dear." And I'm expected to frighten small children—which I often do. I'm permitted all manner of eccentricities and now that I've acquired a cane, can inflict bodily harm with impunity. I've been known to bang it loudly to gain attention and have used it maliciously to destroy offensive objects (and feet). I often eat ice cream for breakfast and take someone else's coat at a party or funeral when I tire of my own. I enjoy making noise, never having done it enough when I was young. I revel in the attention of young people who are always salacious to an elder as spry and spunky as I. I do not suffer the foolish obsessions of the middle aged.

I come to the park to observe the futility of life about me. Experience has relinquished a great secret which I'm not generous enough to share.

## The Boys

Then the boys came, one, two, both pale as milk.

The first a charismatic thug. Cute and endearing, a cherub with rough edges. He's a copy of his father, loving and stubborn. A dirty, sticky boy who embraces and seduces, leaving you slimy, stained and joyful. His high spirits are infectious. His hair grows in wild sweaty curls that must be cut often. He's fond of all creatures especially those who swim the oceans, and he'll lay down in the street to watch a bug scurry along the pavement. The scourge of his big sister's life, he subsists mainly on breakfast foods and awe. He is the most persistent of the descendants.

Boys are more simple than girls. They like things they can pile or line up. Piles and lines are destroyed and remade in an endless cycle. For them, there is order and disorder, serenity and chaos.

They like to see things fly.

## The Sleeping Prince

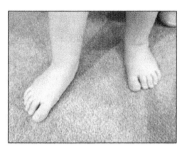 For a while we both had secret names. People know his now though they don't know what he'll want to be called; there are several possibilities. One day I'll tell him my secret name, perhaps today. He slumbers, curled up in his sleep-sack, dreaming of past lives and a life to come. I have much to tell him when he wakes, songs to sing, games to play, more secrets...

Unlike the rest of us, he's blonde with twinkling blue eyes from another realm. He flashes a magnetic grin, a hereditary trait employed to disarm; he sleeps the blameless sleep of monks in unsullied snuggeries. He envies power tools but snuggles a stuffed penguin.

His Familiar—not yet accustomed to new duties—waits with ears erect, and follows each visitor to sniff out their intention.

His room is serene, perfect for sleeping royalty. My kiss doesn't wake him; there is only the taste of manna and the disruption of his wrapping.

## The Dragon Baby

She was born in the windy west of the middle when an errant desert heat hovered over the town like a fiery breath. Villagers came from far and forest to attend the birth and pay homage to an elder brother who drummed time and gabba. The lake was her ocean.

Her mama had been a cowgirl, small and mighty. Her papa

sang ska and loved them all in two languages. Serene grey horizons turned pink with joy. An old house was transformed, a berth for the ancestors secured; relics buried, windows that looked into future were opened. There were feasts and fasts, ritual bathing and offerings.

It's probable that she's the last of an era, that moons will pass, seasons lapse and orbits expand before a new generation arises. This is no cause for lamentation. With her, a great balance has been achieved; two has become four; four, eight and a curse is thwarted; a dynasty set in motion.

## The Snake Baby

In the fierce heat of the Year of the Snake, he slithers between us in spirit. He binds that which is already bound, he gyres among possibilities. He cannot be imagined before his arrival; the world had seemed so set. He is here to remind us that it never is. The circle turns; it expands and contracts. Truth bends to accept the impossible. Arms stretch to embrace a creature of water, a child to fill spaces that we didn't know were empty.

~

# Chapter 26

## Disclaimer

THIS ISN'T THE WHOLE STORY OR THE TRUE STORY. I
NEVER LIE, SING, O GODDESS...

## Author Biography

Gay Partington Terry is a Manx insomniac who grew up in small towns in northern Appalachia. When she was young, she assisted her dad in his magic act. She's been a waitress, factory worker, and welfare worker in northern Appalachia; she catalogued tribal arts for Sotheby's and did volunteer work in Margaret Mead's office and at the Hayden Planetarium.

Her short stories have been published in ezines, anthologies, and fantasy magazines. She helped create the "Toxic Avenger" and wrote parts II and III. Her first book, *Meeting the Dog Girls*, is a collection of short stories.

She has two grown children, two granddaughters, and three grandsons. She's lived in NYC for more than half her life: Greenwich Village, Upper West Side, Chelsea, Brooklyn, and now Harlem. For the sake of sanity (such that it is), she studies tai chi ch'uan, qi gong, and yoga. For the last ten years, she and her husband have been watched over by the ghost of a loyal Australian Shepherd (the dog version).

Learn more at www.gaypartingtonterry.com

Twitter: www.twitter.com/gpterr

✓ ? Sharon : 1) A. Oakley ³⁵ᵗ 77 + 106
2) 71 Melva
3) Prom ✓

p 25 Miss Roland ? ✓ ?M
p 32 Toad ? ?Bar ? ?M
p 32-33 Prom queen ?
✓ ? ever see "Red" p. 47 ? "red"
✓ p 53+ } Ruth Strange  M  ₩ð  OUIJA
    54

  12
    800
  7600
  9600/yr

— p 71 melinda - teacher

— p 60 Howie smoke/anne ?
                      COPD

✓ DIET ? Veg.

✓ ? CBD or ?

Lightning Source UK Ltd.
Milton Keynes UK
UKOW05f2012281116
288751UK00027B/988/P